Supreme Court Great Britain

Instructions to Her Majesty's consular officers in China and Japan

With comments on the China and Japan Order in Council 1865

Supreme Court Great Britain

Instructions to Her Majesty's consular officers in China and Japan
With comments on the China and Japan Order in Council 1865

ISBN/EAN: 9783337173999

Printed in Europe, USA, Canada, Australia, Japan

Cover: Foto ©ninafisch / pixelio.de

More available books at **www.hansebooks.com**

INSTRUCTIONS

TO

HER MAJESTY'S CONSULAR OFFICERS IN CHINA AND JAPAN,

ON THE

MODE OF CONDUCTING JUDICIAL BUSINESS, WITH COMMENTS
ON THE CHINA AND JAPAN ORDER IN COUNCIL 1865,
AND THE RULES OF PROCEDURE FRAMED
UNDER IT.

BY

Sir EDMUND HORNBY, K.t

CHIEF JUDGE OF HER MAJESTY'S SUPREME COURT
FOR CHINA AND JAPAN.

A. H. DE CARVALHO,
SHANGHAI, 1867.

List of the more important Errata.

Page 4, paragraph 6. Place the comma *before* "and in the exercise of it" instead of *after* it.
„ 4, „ 9. For "can so act. Yet it may be doubtful", read "can so act, yet it may be doubtful"
„ 5, „ 5. For "District) are admissible in evidence and no further proof", read "District). No further proof"
„ 9, last line. For "Law—now, Equity", read "Law. Now, Equity"
„ 11, line 10. For "conduct in England", read "conduct. In England"
„ 11, „ 11. Dele "not"
„ 14, „ 13 from foot. After "*Res*" insert "it"
„ 14, last line. For "Material men and persons", read "material men, and persons"
„ 15, „ „ Make "it" commence a new sentence.
„ 17, paragraph 5. Make "any infringement" commence a new sentence.
„ 19, „ 4. Make "it is only against" commence a new sentence.
„ 19, „ 5. Make "the Law against Vagrants" commence a new sentence.
„ 20, line 15. For "nor can we often," read "and, often, we cannot"
„ 23, last paragraph. Make new sentences commence at "all objections" and "the other party"
„ 24, first „ Make new sentences commence at "generally speaking" and "in no case"
„ 26, line 18. For "suit. Sections 1 to 9", read "suit, Rules 1 to 9"
„ 28. For "W. S." in *red* ink, read "S. W."
„ 30, line 13 from foot. Make "the Defendant" commence a new sentence.
„ 33, „ 4. Make a new sentence commence at "it", and read thus—"It is abolished for *debt* under £20; and, when the debt exceeds that sum"
„ 33, last line of par. 3. For "a Referee cannot be", read "no one can be"
„ 37, line 3. Make a new sentence commence at "the Petition"
„ 49, „ 19 from foot. Insert a comma after "hearing"
„ 50, „ 10 „ „ For "delivery", read "delivered"
„ 80, lines 24, 25. Read "A debtor imprisoned for debt, and unable through poverty to pay the expenses attending the filing" &c.
„ 84, line 16. For "or embezzling and part", read "or for embezzling any part"
„ „ „ 4 from foot. Remove comma from after "in" to after "to" in the next line.
„ 93, line 6. Read "The effect of the order of discharge is to release the bankrupt"
„ 96, lines 20, 19, from foot. Read "unprofessional men, should lean rather to the admission of all evidence or testimony which tends" &c.
„ 98, line 15 from foot. Remove comma from after "not unfrequently" to after "Japan"
„ 101, „ 3 of first Notification. For "established" read "establish"
„ 103, „ 12 from foot. Insert "of" before "the contract"
„ 105, „ 9 „ „ Insert "the" before "Judge"

In addition to the above, many typographical errors in punctuation &c. were noted, but too late to permit of convenient correction; nor are they of such importance as to require insertion here.

HER BRITANNIC MAJESTY'S SUPREME COURT FOR CHINA AND JAPAN.

SHANGHAI, 1st *January*, 1867.

To H. M.'s CONSULS *in China & Japan.*

GENTLEMEN,

I have had it in contemplation for some time past to address you on the subject of the performance by you of your judicial duties. Hitherto I have been prevented from doing so by my time having been taken up in superintending the first establishment of the Supreme Court at Shanghai. I do not now propose to write an essay on the whole duties of Consuls, but simply to draw your attention to the mode in which you should act in the exercise of the jurisdiction conferred on you by the "Order in Council for China and Japan 1865," and I beg you to remember that this is not a letter addressed to any one of you in particular, but collectively to a body of Gentlemen who have greater or less experience in the performance of their Consular duties, and greater or less knowledge of the subject to which it refers. I remind you of this because to be useful to all, it is necessary for me to assume that some have little or no knowledge of how those duties are, or ought to be performed. This is my reason for treating the subject in a very elementary manner. I do not for a moment imagine but that many of you have no need of the instruction or information which I design to convey, but because some of you are perfectly equal to the proper discharge of your duties, this of itself is no reason why the ignorance of others should not be provided for.

First let me observe that some knowledge of the constitution of our country and of the Laws which are framed to guide the conduct of its citizens, should not be confined to Lawyers, but should be considered as absolutely essential to the education of every English Gentleman, and if this is true, it is needless to remark how much more essential such knowledge becomes when English Gentlemen are called upon to administer these Laws. No one expects from you perfect knowledge on such a subject. Men who have devoted their lives to its acquirement seldom, if ever have attained it—but *this* is expected of you, viz: that you should have an elementary knowledge of the first Principles which pervade the whole system of our Law —that you should know where to find the Law as laid down by Statutes—or where mentioned and commented on by text-writers, and that you should bring to its consideration and administration a fair amount of industry, common sense and, above all, perfect impartiality in its application.

Besides the Municipal Law of England or in other words, that Law which is confined to the realm of England and to those who live within it—there is another system of Law with which it particularly behoves Consular Officers to have some acquaintance.

I allude to International Law—that is, that system of Law which guides the relations of nations in their dealings with each other—and that branch of it which treats of the rights and obligations which the Citizens of one State bear towards the Government of another State—and *vice versa*. This International Law is so eminently the offspring of the sense of what is mutually fair and right, that its principles recommend themselves to the mind as the natural result of the moral rule "do unto others as you would be done by" and the perusal of such works as those of Mr. Wheaton and Dr. Phillimore should be undertaken less as a task than as a recreation. A single careful reading of either of these works will prevent Consuls from falling into many errors and will intuitively free them from many prejudices which spring from too exclusive a consideration of private national interests.

I recommend all Consular Officers who seek to rise in their career —or, to take a higher ground—are, as they should all be, anxious to perform their duties conscientiously, to devote some time to the study of "Stephen's Blackstone's Commentaries," the last Edition of "Smith's Mercantile Law," "Chitty on Contracts," "Arnould on Marine Insurance," "Byles on Bills of Exchange," "Taylor on evidence" and "Roscoe's Criminal Law."

In "Stephen's Blackstone" the Student will find a general outline of the Civil and Criminal Law and having made himself Master of the contents of this invaluable work, which may be said to set forth the principles which permeate every branch of our legal system, he will come to the study of the other works I have mentioned with a mind prepared to understand and appreciate them.

These should be read carefully, but no great effort need be made to burden the memory with their contents. Law is not one of those sciences which in its elementary study demands an accurate recollection of every formula. What the Student should endeavour to attain to is a knowledge of principles, and to know where to find the Law.

I mention this, because nothing serves to frighten Students of Law so much as the supposed necessity of burdening their memories with the mass of cases which are quoted in our text Books or with the infinite number of Statutes which fill up the book-shelves of every Lawyer's Chambers.

The most that a Consul can be expected to know is, where to find the Law on any of the matters most likely to come under his notice and to apply it fairly and correctly, but unless he follow the advice I have ventured to offer he is not very likely to be able to do the one or the other.

So imperative has the necessity become of those who are called upon to administer the Law having some knowledge of it, that I believe it is not unlikely Consular Officers will be required to pass an Examination in different branches of Law, and in the Rules of Procedure, before being appointed or promoted to any Post where they are to exercise magisterial or judicial functions.

I have reprinted the Circular Letter which I addressed to Her Majesty's Consular Officers in the Levant, after having re-arranged and adapted it to the circumstances attending the exercise of judicial duties by Consular Officers in China and Japan, and as it gives an outline of the mode, in which judicial proceedings should be conducted, I trust it will be found useful; but to be so something more than a hasty perusal of it, is requisite.

I can easily conceive that it does not present matter of very interesting study—and the same may be said of what I am now writing—but unless Consular Officers prefer to master the sources whence the information both contain, are derived—it is absolutely essential they should make themselves familiarly acquainted with what is after all but a very meagre outline.

With these observations I pass to the consideration of the Order in Council.

By the ninth paragraph of the Preamble you will observe that several Consular Ordinances—mentioned in the Schedule of the Order—are repealed—but there is a class of Orders that refer to Shipping and to Harbour Regulations at several of the Treaty Ports which still remain in force, these not being affected by the Order—except in so far as they are in contradiction with it. *Preamble to Order in Council—what Orders repealed.*

In future however, it will not be competent for Consuls of their own motion to enact ordinances—or to make Rules of Procedure and with the exception of those which have been or may be approved and sanctioned by the Minister or Judge of the Supreme Court respectively, the rest will have no force or effect. *Consuls not to enact Ordinances.*

I mention this, because it has been somewhat hastily assumed, that all the Rules existing at the time of the present Order in Council coming into force, were repealed by it and the consequence has been that confusion has resulted, which a more careful consideration of the Order would have avoided.

No jurisdiction should be exercised under the 3rd Section over a Naturalized British Subject in the place where there is a Consul of the Nationality of the Country of his Birth, until such Consul shall have been communicated with and repudiated all jurisdiction over him. *Naturalized British Subjects.*

A Person of the Chinese Race born in a British Possession of Parents who were also born there is undoubtedly a British Subject, and so are Children born in such possessions of Chinese Parents who have been there naturalized; but as against the Authorities of China Children of Chinese Parents who were themselves not naturalized or born British Subjects are not entitled *in China* to be considered or treated as British Subjects notwithstanding they may have been born in a British Colony or Possession. This Rule has been wisely laid down by H. M.'s Government to prevent in China the abuse of the Rules of English Law on the subject of Birth conferring citizenship, which would in all probability occur if Chinese Subjects could obtain for their Children the Status of British-born subjects by simply providing for their birth taking place on the soil of a British Possession. *Persons of the Chinese Race, born or Naturalized in a British Possession.*

Chinese naturalized in a British Colony or Possession can claim no rights as British Subjects beyond the limits of such Colony or Possession. The moment they enter China, their allegiance to the Sovereign of China revives.

The same Rules will doubtless be held applicable to Japan.

It follows from what has been said, that if a Person of Chinese Race is a British Subject, he is entitled to the Privileges and must submit to the disabilities arising out of that character. Those privileges are defined by Treaty, and if a Native-born Englishman of the Anglo-Saxon race cannot reside permanently in the interior of China,—cannot travel without a Passport—cannot buy, or inherit Landed Property,—cannot own a Chinese Ship, neither can a British Subject of the Chinese Race.

Foreigners borne on the Muster Roll of a Ship.

In the second Paragraph of the same Section which makes mention of Foreigners, it is to be remembered that Foreigners borne on the Muster Roll of a British Vessel are to be considered quoad all that regards the Ship, its discipline and Crew as amenable to British Consular jurisdiction, but if a Foreigner so borne on the Roll of a British Ship, commits an Offence or Crime on shore, such act having nothing to do with the Ship or his character of a Seaman under the British Flag, he will be amenable to the jurisdiction of the Consul of the Country of his Birth.

How Jurisdiction to be exercised.

The 4th, 5th and 6th Sections of the Order require little or no explanation. They simply declare that all the jurisdiction conferred by the Order is to be exercised according to its provisions—that the Law to be enforced is the Law of England and that no act is to be deemed a Criminal Act (except it be one expressly made Criminal by the Order) that is not a Criminal Act according to the Law of England.

Meaning of words "Circumstances will admit" in 5th Section of Order.

By the words "Circumstances will admit" in the 5th Section is meant, that unless there is some positive reason to the contrary amounting to "inability to administer the Law of England in its integrity," such Law is to be the guide and basis of every act and decision of a Consular Authority.

Merchant Shipping Act.

Although no specific mention is made in the 5th Section, as in former Orders in Council of the jurisdiction of Consuls under the Merchant Shipping Act, yet under this Section such jurisdiction is in fact continued in them and in the exercise of it, they must conform to the Instructions issued by the Board of Trade.

Sections 7 to 24 inclusive have special reference to the Supreme Court.

What Consular Officers can hold Courts.

The only observation that Section 25th requires is that no Consular Officer who has not a Commission from Her Majesty can hold a Consular Court, and it follows that the Representative of a non-Commissioned Consular Officer is equally disqualified.

This Section does not affect Consular Agents who are not generally Commissioned Officers nor can they be considered as the Representatives of the Consuls from whom they depend and in whose district they act, so as to bring them within the meaning of that portion of the Section which alludes to persons acting temporarily as and for a Consular Officer. They cannot therefore hold a Consular Court. Although a person—acting temporarily with the approval of the Secretary of State or of Her Majesty's Minister—can so act. Yet it may be doubtful whether under the 19th Section of the 12 and 13 Vict. Ch. 68, "any person duly authorized to act in the absence of such Consul," can marry persons, inasmuch as the authority

to marry is conferred on the individual Consul himself, by an express authorization in writing which authority it might be contended did not pass to or devolve on the temporary Representative.

Sections 26 to 32 refer to "Juries." At present no case can be tried in a Provincial Consular Court by a Jury—Section 62 practically limiting this form of trial to the Supreme Court until it shall please one of Her Majesty's Secretaries of State to extent it to Provincial Courts. It is however the duty of Consuls to prepare Jury lists in accordance with the Order, and to send them when revised and settled to the Chief Judge of the Supreme Court, as in the event of any Judicial Officer of the Supreme Court visiting a Provincial Court for the purpose of hearing any suit or trying any Prisoners, it is from this list that the Jurors would have to be drawn. A Copy should also be forwarded to the Secretary of State for the purpose of enabling him to act under the 62nd Section. Juries.

Under the 33rd and 34th Section, I need not perhaps remark that Consuls have no power to compel the attendance of Assessors, and when these latter refuse, or neglect, to comply with a Summons, the Consul should proceed to the hearing and determination of the case, noting on the face of the proceedings the fact of the Summons and the refusal or neglect to attend on the part of the Assessors. Assessors.

The 63rd Section has also reference to Assessors.

Subdivision V. of the Order defining the jurisdiction and authority of Her Majesty's Courts is of the greatest importance, and Consuls should make themselves thoroughly acquainted with it as it is the source whence they derive their jurisdiction in their several Courts. Jurisdiction of Courts.

All Consular, or in other words Provincial Courts, are Courts of Record—that is to say all proceedings before them are matter of Record and are admitted in evidence when occasion requires upon a simple exhibition of the Record—in other words the written proceedings—sealed with the Seal of the Court (which until a new Seal is approved by one of the Secretaries of State will be the Seal of the Consulate of the District) are admissible in evidence and no further proof of their authenticity is requisite. But this very provision shows the importance as well as necessity of Consuls keeping a full and accurate Record of the Proceedings in every case, and no neglect in this respect can be excused, because the omission may seriously prejudice the rights and interests of the parties to a suit, and disable them from establishing facts which have been admitted or proved, or from prosecuting an appeal. What Courts of Record.

The Supreme Court has an extraordinary original jurisdiction over the whole of China and Japan concurrently with the jurisdiction of the several Provincial Courts—that is, it can take cognizance of any case in any Consular District and act as if it were actually for the time being established within such District. Its Judges can either visit a Provincial Court and hear any case arising within its District, or the Chief Judge can order any case which he considers fit to be heard and determined by the Supreme Court, to be sent up for that purpose to Shanghai. Concurrent Jurisdiction of Supreme Court with Provincial Courts.

But because this Authority has been conferred on the Judge of the Supreme Court, it does not follow that it will be often exercised. The business of the Court at Shanghai is too important and too great to enable its Judges to be absent or to undertake the determination of cases in the first instance arising in another Consular District. Each Consul is bound to hear and determine every case arising within his peculiar jurisdiction and with as much promptitude as a careful compliance with the Rules of Procedure permit. It is only in those cases where the questions involved are of great importance and the solution of them of great difficulty, that the Supreme Court will exercise its right of concurrent jurisdiction and in no case will it hear a part heard case. On more than one occasion a case has been sent up to the Supreme Court simply because in the course of the hearing before the Court below, points of difficulty have arisen which the Consul has not thought himself competent to decide, and the case has been sent back occasioning great expense and delay.

Special Cases.
The Rules of Procedure *(See Rule 99)* provide sufficiently for the submission of special cases involving one or more points of Law or fact; but even the assistance thus afforded should not be hastily invoked. It is the duty of every Judicial Officer to do his best to come to a decision upon any point one way or the other, and nothing is so calculated to incapacitate a man for the proper performance of his duties as the habit of evading a difficulty by an immediate reference of it to some one else.

Execution by Provincial Courts of Writs, &c.
The 43rd, 44th and 46th Sections confer considerable power and entail some responsibility, and i n acting under them Consuls will do well to confine themselves strictly to fulfilling the terms of the Writ and Warrant. In cases where it is left optional to them to take security for the appearance of the person named, care should be taken that the Security demanded be not excessive in amount, and as a general rule, the Security of third persons conjointly with that of the Person himself is to be preferred to that of the personal security of the individual alone—but where it is impossible for collateral security to be found—some more tangible security than a recognizance, or mere promise to pay some sum of money, should be taken. Consuls however, are supposed to have more or less some personal knowledge of the means, character and circumstances of individual Englishmen residing within their districts, and by that knowledge they must to a considerable extent be governed.

Courts auxiliary to each other.
Some confusion has arisen from the different interpretations which have been given to the 46th Section which declares that all Courts in China and Japan shall be auxiliary to one another. It is not however meant by this Section that the different Courts are to travel out of their respective jurisdictions or blindly acquiesce in any request that may be made to them. Thus, to take an instance that has occurred where both of the Consular Officers ostensibly acting under this Section, did wrong—a Plaintiff began an action in the Consular Court of A, against a Defendant residing and carrying on business in B, and the Consul of A, sent his Summons to the Defendant to appear and answer the plaint in A, the Summons he enclosed in a letter to the Consul of B, and the Consul of B caused it to be served on the Defendant and in compliance with the request enclosed in the letter demanded and took Security from the Defendant for his appearance at A, at the time mentioned in the Summons.—Here

both Consuls were wrong. The Consul of A should not, except under very particular circumstances—such as the absconding of a Defendant to avoid service of a Summons—summon a man from another Consular district to appear before him. It is the business of a Plaintiff to follow a Defendant and it is no part of the duty of a Consul to summon a Defendant residing in another district simply because it suits the Plaintiff's convenience that he should be so summoned.

In most cases by making use of the Provisions in the Rules (*See Rules* 254 *to* 259) for service at the last place of residence, &c., &c., a Plaintiff will obtain all that he requires, because he will be enabled to proceed to judgment in the absence of the Defendant. But Consuls must be extremely careful, in dispensing with personal service and should only do so in very clear cases and where it is essential to the ends of justice. In Cases of Service.

And when the circumstances justify the issuing of a Summons under Rule 257 into another district it should only issue in accordance with a judicial Order made upon a regular application supported by facts deposed to on Oath—all of which should remain matter of Record. The Consul of B in the case alluded to was wrong in acting on a simple request—it ought to have been officially made and under the Seal of the Court of A, and not being so made he should not have acted upon it. As a general rule it will be as well for a Consul who is asked to issue a Summons into another District to suspend his acquiescence until he shall have had time to ask the opinion of the Judge of the Supreme Court—but there may be cases of urgency when he will have to act on his own judgment and responsibility.

He will then do well to satisfy himself first—that the Plaintiff has a good cause of action—that the demand is a liquidated demand and not a simple claim sounding in damages. Secondly, that there is some better reason than that of the Plaintiff's convenience for his not going himself or appointing some one to represent him in the District in which the Defendant is and in which in strictness the case should be tried—and thirdly, it is generally adviseable that the Plaintiff should be called on to give some good and sufficient security to answer any action which the Defendant may bring against him to recover such damages as he may have sustained by being improperly brought up—and the Consul to whom the request is made should make an Order for service (*See Rule* 257) in something like the following form:—

"In Her Britannic Majesty's Consular Court at Chefoo.

A. B.—Plaintiff

"Between

C. D.—Defendant

"At the request of the Consular Court of Hankow I do order that "service of the Summons in this Suit be effected on the Defendant.

E. F.

| Consular Seal. |

Vice-Consul

Chefoo."

Execution may issue to Provincial Court from Supreme Court.

By Section 43—Execution may issue from the Supreme Court to a Provincial Court to seize and sell in satisfaction of a judgment obtained in the Supreme Court, the goods of a Defendant within the jurisdiction of the Provincial Court.

A Warrant of Execution will however only issue on an Order made by the Supreme Court on a motion by the Plaintiffs supported by an Affidavit of such facts as will justify the Court in granting it, and on Security being given to answer any damages that may be sustained by the Consul in the Execution of the Warrant. A Consul on receiving the Warrant will put it in Execution and having so acted upon it will endorse on it the amount of the Levy and return it with such amount to the Supreme Court.

There are however, many ways in which Courts may be properly made auxiliary to each other. Thus, in securing the Estates of deceased British Subjects, in taking possession of and selling the property of a Bankrupt at the request of the Official Assignee—in serving notices on next of kin and Creditors—and in procuring information upon an infinite variety of subjects connected with the administration of Justice.

Half-yearly Return.

In accordance with the 47th Section, Consuls should on the 1st of July and on the 1st of January of every year, report on the cases that have been tried in their Consular Courts. The Form of this Report should be as follows:—

"Half-yearly Return of cases (Civil) tried in Her Britannic Majesty's

"Consular Court at   from the 1st of January to 30th

"of June."

Name of Plaintiff.	Name of Defendant.	Date of Filing Petition.	Date of Hearing.	How disposed of.

Fees paid _____

The same Form will apply to Criminal and Police cases the return of which is to be made up separately. They should be addressed to the Chief Judge of the Supreme Court, and any observations that Consuls may consider necessary upon any case should accompany them.

Reconciliation Clauses.

I pass now to the Sections empowering Courts to promote reconciliation and facilitate the settlement in an amicable way of any proceeding before it.

Perhaps no Sections in the Order in Council have been less understood and because often mis-understood have led to greater inconvenience—yet it is hardly possible to conceive that any language could be clearer than that employed. In the first place—those Sections are confined to "*Civil Matters*"—Secondly a Suit *must* be *pending.*

It is not intended that on a difference of opinion arising between British Subjects as to their mutual rights or obligations, a Consul is to put himself forward and endeavour by the exercise of personal influence to bring the parties to an arrangement. But what he may do is this: On a suit being commenced in his Court—or even under the 143rd Section without recourse being had to litigation—and on a proper opportunity arising, and when the parties are before him, a Consul may without expressing any opinion on the merits—suggest that the case is one that had better be settled amicably—either in or out of Court—but he should not argue the case on its merits with either one or other of the parties in order to induce them to consent to an amicable settlement; for, in doing so, he may be prejudging a case he has not fully heard, which after all he may be compelled to hear, or be intimating an opinion on matters with which he is not acquainted and which it may be necessary to take evidence to arrive at, and by such prejudgment or intimation he is putting a pressure on the party against whom the inclination of his opinion runs, to do that which he may not feel inclined to do, and which if done at all, should be a purely voluntary act.

All a Consul should do,—if he conceives it to be for the interest of both parties—is simply to suggest the reasons why an amicable arrangement should be come to and it is not until the parties are agreed to an amicable arrangement instead of a judicial decision, that the terms of the arrangement should be discussed and even then, the Consul is not the person to discuss them—but the parties themselves. Although if the matter is by the consent of the parties referred to the Consul, he may determine it—noting on the proceedings and in his Note-Book the fact of the reference to himself and the decision he has arrived at. Reference to Consuls.

So with regard to Arbitration—A Suit must be commenced before it can be referred. A reference then becomes a Judicial Order in the proceedings made by consent and is a matter of Record—or in the case of Accounts (*See Rule* 59) without consent—and it must be conducted in conformity with Sections 49 and 50 of the Order and with Rules 217 to 229. Arbitration.

Provincial Courts are Courts of Law and equity—they have a jurisdiction in Bankruptcy and Consuls can act as Coroners. A Provincial Court can also grant a Probate or administration when there is no contention as to the grant and when the deceased had his fixed place of abode within its jurisdiction. Courts of Law and Equity. Bankruptcy. Coroner's Courts. Probate Courts.

The Supreme Court can alone exercise a jurisdiction in Admiralty—in Lunacy, in Matrimonial cases and in contentious cases of Probate and Administration. Supreme Court alone a Court of Admiralty can alone act in matters of Lunacy. Matrimonial Cases—and Contentious Probate Cases.

There is a good deal of mis-apprehension as to the character of a Court of Equity. By many persons it is supposed to be a Court which ignores Law and rests its decisions upon the ideas of natural reason and justice which its Judge for the time being may happen to entertain. Nothing is so common as for Suitors to say "We don't want Law—we want equity"—and Consuls not unfrequently fall into the same error and apologise for any defect in their judgments by saying that they preferred to decide the case before them equitably rather than by any rules of Law—now, Equity is a branch of Law What is Equity.

just as much as the Criminal Law or the Law of Bankruptcy is a branch of the general Law of England. It is governed by certain known rules, and whatever it may have been in its origen, its Courts administer a system of Laws as complete as those which govern the decisions of the Courts of Common Law. Therefore it is a mistake to suppose that a Judge sitting in Equity is to disregard the principles by which Courts of Equity are governed, and simply to decide the case before him by his own unassisted ideas of what may be fair or right. A careful study of those Chapters of Stephen's Blackstone which treat of equitable jurisdiction will best serve to dissipate the somewhat perverse notions that prevail on this subject.

The Law of Bankruptcy is in a transition state. The Legislature and the Mercantile Classes are in doubt as to the exact form which legislation should take with reference to it. But, whatever course is adopted, this it is sufficient for Consuls to know, that it is and will be exactly defined by Statute.

Bankruptcy Law is so essentially the creature of an artificial state of Society that it must necessarily be governed by distinct and special enactments and to them alone it will be necessary for Consuls to refer for guidance. There are however certain general principles to which it may be as well to allude. No Bankrupt Law is intended or ever will be intended to enable a fraudulent Debtor to escape the just punishment due to unfair dealing—neither is it, or will it be intended to enable a man to dispose of his property—then get a discharge from his liabilities and begin the world again as a perfectly free man. The moment a man finds himself in difficulties of such a nature that it is extremely improbable any amount of labour, or any temporary assistance that he may possible obtain, will relieve him from them, it is his duty to avail himself of the Law of Bankruptcy and if he neglects to avail himself of it, it is the duty of a Court of Bankruptcy whenever he appears before it to mark its sense of such neglect by suspending for a greater or less period its Order of Discharge. In the same way it is the duty of a Judge in Bankruptcy to put in force what are called the Criminal Sections of the Bankruptcy Law whenever the occasion calls for it. Such severity is as necessary for the safety of honest traders as for the punishment of improvident and fraudulent Bankrupts. It is a very common thing for men to continue trading when they know themselves to be in a state of hopeless insolvency. They buy on credit, trusting to sell for cash at a profit, and thus, to use a common phrase, to keep the Mill going—and when this is no longer possible, they pay such of their Creditors as are most importunate or let actions be brought against them and defend them, knowing perfectly that they have no defence, nor assets to satisfy an execution issued under any judgment that may be obtained against them—or they do what perhaps is worse, they pay some Creditors in full and leave the rest wholly unpaid—they then appear in a Bankruptcy Court or are brought into it without a farthing upon which a dividend might be declared.

This is Mercantile dishonesty and as such punishable. The dividend which Bankrupt Estates can pay, is often no unfair criterion —in nine cases out of ten it is a very fair one—of the Bankrupt's conduct as a Debtor, and may serve in many cases to guide a Consul

in considering when and how he should grant him a discharge from his liabilities. There are of course many cases where it will be a most fallacious test—unforeseen misfortune—the conduct of others—may combine to the ruin of a Man, and each case ought to be taken on its own merits, and in all cases the interests and wishes of the mainbody of the Creditors should be regarded; but it by no means follows because the Creditors are careless and supine, which when they know there is no Estate to divide amongst them they often are,—that the Court should neglect its duty and fail to mark its own opinion of a Bankrupt's conduct in England a great deal may be left to Creditors—but not in China and Japan where a Man's Creditors generally include a number of Foreigners ignorant of our Laws and Procedure, it is for the credit of the English name and in the end for the benefit of English Commerce that this ignorance or indifference should not serve as an excuse for the escape of a fraudulent Debtor from the just punishment of his Offences. It would be far better to have no Bankruptcy Law, and leave every man to the mercy of his Creditors than to allow it to be abused to the exclusive advantage of persons who think that when they are unable to pay what they owe—no matter how their obligations were incurred, they have but to apply to a Court of Bankruptcy to obtain their discharge, and snap their fingers at their Creditors.

A Bankrupt must find the means to pay all the fees and other expenses incident to his Bankruptcy—he has no right to throw this burden upon his assignees except they have assets in their hands—neither can he properly escape such payment as he cannot petition the Court "in formâ pauperis"—unless he is in Prison at the suit of a creditor. He is then adjudicated a Bankrupt by the Registrar of the Court—under the 98th and following secs. of the Bankrupt Act of 1861 and a Consul can himself act as Registrar.

It is almost needless to remark that the times, prescribed by the act, within which certain steps in Bankruptcy have to be taken, must be adhered to. It is always in the power of the Court to adjourn a sitting, pro formâ, but every endeavour must be made to hold the regular sittings, and give the requisite notices ordered by the act at the periods mentioned therein.

I would especially draw the attention of Consuls to the short sketch of the Bankruptcy Acts in the accompanying Extract from the "Levant Consular Letter," at the same time cautioning them not to rule themselves entirely by what is there laid down, but always to seek confirmation of what is there said, in the Acts themselves. (*See also* Stephen's Blackstone P. 145 et seq.)

In their capacity of Coroners, Consuls will do well to remember that every case of sudden death unless the cause is what may be termed a natural cause, and it is certified by a duly qualified and respectable Medical man, is a fit case for an inquest. I do not mean to say that a Consul should insist upon holding an inquest upon every case of sudden death unless there are grounds for suspecting that either gross carelessness or actual violence has been the cause of it. Inquests must always be held on view of the body, and by a Jury of not less than three persons. And for the purposes of an

Coroners.

inquest a Consul may summon any three or more persons comprised in the ordinary Jury list of the Court.

The Jury are to be sworn to inquire into and give a verdict expressive of their opinion on the evidence brought before them of how and when the deceased came by his death. In these, as in all other cases, the Consul should keep a Note-Book in which to enter the particulars—the evidence adduced—and the finding of the Jury. Where there are Medical men attached to the Consulates paid by a Salary—their evidence as to the cause of death should be given and given gratuitously, but where it is necessary to make a Post-mortem examination, a fee of three and in some case five Pounds is usually given. These fees should be defrayed from any Property which the deceased may have possessed—but if he has none, and the Post-mortem has not been made at the request of any Relative—in which case the expense should be borne by him—then it should be charged in the Consular accounts to Government. The Jury are not entitled to any remuneration.

On the finding of a dead body of a Native or a Foreigner in the employment of a British Subject, or where there is any suspicion or reason to suspect that a British Subject may be in a greater or less degree involved in the circumstances attending the death of the deceased—the Consul should either himself attend to view the body, or delegate this task to an intelligent Assistant—a Medical man should also be, where it is possible, in attendance.

This is a measure of precaution and as necessary to protect the innocent as to punish the guilty. On more than one occasion it has happened to me to be overwhelmed with evidence of a Body presenting marks of violence going directly to fix a British Subject who had been known to strike the deceased in whose employ he was, as having caused or been accessory to the death, a conclusion which could have been easily negatived if a Medical man or even an ordinarily intelligent European had seen the body.

In one case, it was only, on a strict cross-examination, that I found myself forced to conduct, I elicited, first, that the deceased had been some days before his death engaged in a gambling row where he had been beaten, and that his body moreover had been in the Water amongst the Shipping for six days—had it not been for these facts thus with difficulty elicited, the weight of evidence would have been sadly against the Englishman who long after the time when, if found guilty, he would have been hanged, was proved to have had literally nothing to do with the death of the deceased.

The Jury should be sworn.
The following forms of Summons and Oath may be used.
Provincial Court of   }   To the Constable
                          }   of   .   .   .   .   .
These are in Her Majesty's name to command you immediately to summon three persons whose names are on the Jury list of this Court to appear before me   Judge of the Provincial Court of   on the   day of   at   o'clock in the   noon to inquire concerning the death of

(Sealed with the Seal of the Court.)

You shall deligently inquire and true presentment make how *Oath to Jury.*
A. D. (or a person unknown) now lying dead, came to his death
and of such other matters relating to the same, as shall lawfully be
required of you according to the evidence you shall receive.

"So help you God."

Having administered this Oath the Coroner will proceed with the
Jury to view the body. If a Medical man is at hand, he should go
with the Jury and examine the body if no examination has previously been made. The Coroner and Jury having seen the body and
taken note of any particular circumstances as wounds, &c., &c., will
proceed to hear such evidence as may be forthcoming.

The Oath administered to a Witness may be as follows. "The *Oath of Witness.*
"evidence you shall give to this Inquest touching the death of
"A. D. shall be the truth the whole truth and nothing but the
"truth."

"So help you God."

The Coroner must hear all evidence that is offered and that upon
Oath. A party accused of murder or against whom suspicion arises,
may bring evidence if he can in his on behalf.

The Coroner has power to compel the attendance of all British
Subjects as witnesses, and to commit them for contempt if they
refuse to appear. On the appearance of a witness the Coroner
should take down his name, abode and occupation and then administer the Oath. Chinese, Malays, Roman Catholics and persons
of other religions may be sworn according to their own customs.

The Coroner must put the evidence of the witnesses in writing
or as much of it as is material—and in case any one appears to
have been guilty of manslaughter or murder he must bind by
recognisance all witnesses if they be British Subjects, who have
any evidence to give, to appear when the party charged shall be
prosecuted for the same, and if they are Foreigners, application
should be made to their respective national Authorities to secure
their attendance at the trial.

The Coroner should seal and subscribe the note of the evidence
taken and the inquisition, and deliver the same to the proper Officer
of the Court before which the offender is to be tried.

The examination of witnesses is to be taken down as nearly as
possible in the words of the witnesses and not according to the
effect simply.

If the place where the body is, be inconvenient for the purpose of
holding an inquest, the Coroner may adjourn it to another time or
another place.

The verdict of the Jury should state as plainly and simply as *Verdict of Jury.*
possible the facts of the case—showing the manner—wherein or
cause whereby or by what means the deceased came by his death.
Immediately after the Jury have pronounced their verdict—it should
be put in writing. The Coroner and Jurors must sign the inquisition. The signatures should be in full stating both Christian and
surname of each juror.

Form of an Inquisition.

Form of Inquisition.

FOOCHOW { An inquisition taken at (the Police Station or as the case may be) in Foochow aforesaid the   day of   1866, before A. B.

Her Britannic Majesty's Consul at Foochow, acting as Coroner in accordance with the 53rd Section of the China and Japan Order in Council 1865 upon view of the body of M. N. at No. 100. Street in Foochow aforesaid there and now lying dead upon the Oaths of C. D., E. F. and G. H. (jurors) the several persons whose names are hereunder written good and lawful men of Foochow aforesaid, who being now here sworn and charged to inquire on the part of Our Lady the Queen when, where, how and by what means the said M. N. came to his death do upon their Oaths say that (X. Y. now in custody of the Police did on the   day of   in the year aforesaid feloniously wilfully and of his malice aforethought kill and murder the said M. N.) against the peace of Our Lady the Queen her Crown and dignity.

In witness whereof as well the said Coroner as the Jurors aforesaid have hereunto subscribed their names the day and year above written.

Consul and Coroner.

Jurors { C. D.
         E. F.
         G. H.

Admiralty.

Consuls will observe that by the 54th Section an Admiralty jurisdiction has been specially conferred on the Supreme Court, and on that Court alone. This jurisdiction is an exceptional one in many respects, and although no Provincial Court has power to exercise it, yet it is necessary that Consuls should make themselves acquainted with its nature, and bear it in mind so as to enable them to advise parties having claims against a Ship as to their remedies and the means of recovering them in the Supreme Court. It is an essential, and it may almost be called a peculiar feature of Admiralty jurisdiction that it may be exercised, and most usually is exercised, not against the Owners personally but against the Ship itself—its Apparel and even its Cargo. The Procedure indeed provides for any parties interested in the Ship or Cargo to come in and release the *Res* as is called by giving Bail and entering an appearance—but it is essentially against the Ship, &c., that the action is instituted.

Claims for Seaman's wages
—for Master's wages and for his Disbursements on account of the Ship
—in respect of Pilotage, Tonnage, Salvage of any Ship, or of Life or Goods therefrom
—of damage done by any Ship, Claims of Bottomery, or Respondentia Bonds
—of any Mortgage when the Ship has been sold by a Decree of a Vice-Admiralty Court and the proceeds

are under its controul, are generally enforced under this jurisdiction, and although in England Material men and persons who

have repaired a Ship, except they continue in possession of her, have no maritime Lien on an English Vessel in an English Port yet by the Vice-Admiralty Court Act 1863, i. e. 26 and 27 Vict. Ch. 24 Sec. 10 claims for necessaries, building, equipping or reparing a Vessel within any British possession where no Owner or part Owner is domiciled, are admitted and can be recovered in a Vice-Admiralty Court in an action in *Rem* against the Ship, and as by the Order in Council Section 54 which I have referred to, the Supreme Court in China and Japan has all such jurisdiction as belongs to the Admiralty Courts in Her Majesty's possessions abroad, it would seem to follow that the provisions of the Act of 1863 are equally applicable to the Supreme Court.

The proceedings to be taken on the death of a British Subject are discribed with sufficient clearness in Sections 57 to 61, and in Rules 184 to 216 and all I need I think observe with reference to them, is, that the personal property of a deceased British Subject, vests exclusively under the 59th Section until Probate is taken out or administration granted, in the Judge of the Supreme Court and in no one else, and that consequently no one has any right to interfere with, or exercise controul over such property, other than one of Her Majesty's Consular Officers, and he can only do so in accordance with the Orders of the Judge of the Supreme Court. *Proceedings on Death.*

In cases where there are no fit Guardians of the Property left, or where there is reason to suppose it may be dissipated or stolen—or where the interests of those in whose possession it may be, are exactly at variance with those of the Relatives or Creditors of the deceased—it is the duty of the Consul to take actual possession of it himself or after taking an accurate inventory of it, to leave some one in possession—or he may leave the party in whose actual custody it happens to be in possession, on his giving sufficient security to be answerable for it. The Consul should then immediately communicate to the Judge of the Supreme Court the course he has taken, and ask for instructions, giving him at the same time such particulars of the Estate and of the Persons entitled to it, as can be obtained. But some tact and a sincere desire not to act so as to wound the sensibilities of surviving relatives or friends, is absolutely necessary. Thus, when there is a Wife or Children left, or any very near relatives absolute possession should not be taken, nor indeed should any immediate steps be taken except affixing a notice of the death in the Public Office of the Consulate. Within, however, a reasonable time the provisions of the Order in Council should be considerably brought to the notice of the Survivors, and the proper steps be taken for the grant of Probate or Administration. No Consular Officer however, can erect himself into an Official Administrator of a deceased person's Estate—such an appointment can only be made by the Judge of the Supreme Court and will only be made when it is perfectly evident that there is no other fit or proper person to perform the Office. *Official Administration.*

The power of granting Probate or Letters of Administration conferred on the Supreme Court and (with a limitation) on Provincial Courts, is confined to the Wills and Estates of Persons "having at the time of death their fixed places of abode in China or Japan," it *Probate.*

would seem to follow therefore that the property of a person dying in either Country—*not* having a fixed place of abode therein, may be made over to any person properly authorized by a grant of Probate and Administration obtained from any other Probate Court within whose jurisdiction the deceased had his place of permanent residence or where the Bulk of his property was—without Probate or Administration being first obtained in the Court of the district in which the party died. In such cases the original Probate or Letters of Administration should be produced to the Consul, and he should stamp them with the Seal of his Court and require a Copy of them to be deposited with himself.

Death elsewhere than in China or Japan.

Cases may also occur where the ordinary residence of the deceased has been in China and Japan for some years preceding his death, but from some circumstances Probate of his Will or Letters of Administration to his effects may have been granted in England, Hongkong or elsewhere. Such Probates or Letters of Administration, provided no Will of subsequent date be found here, should be recognized and the course of proceeding will be the same as in the other case; but it is not in general expedient that a Consular Officer should thus part with the property of a Deceased British Subject until he has first consulted the Judge of the Supreme Court on the subject.

When a Partner dies.

In the case of Partners, it is the duty of the surviving Partners to close the Books of the Firm as far as can be done and open new ones in respect of every transaction subsequent to the death, and in the absence of any Legal representative the Consul should inform the surviving Partners of their duty in this respect and require from them a statement of the actual amount of interest which the deceased had in the Partnership stock and effects at the time of his death. And this statement with all the particulars that can be collected relative to the deceased—his relations and his property, should be immediately forwarded to the Judge of the Supreme Court who will give the necessary instructions. But in Partnership Estates it must be recollected Partners have only undivided shares or interests in the whole and until conversion there is no separate Estate, so that on the death of a Partner, his surviving associates become the Trustees of his share and hold the same to the use of his relatives or next of kin—thus this holding possession is not considered as and does not fall under the provision of the 60th Section, and the surviving Partners are not liable to the penalties mentioned therein.

Administration.

As regards Administration where no opposition is made to the application it must be borne in mind that the next of kin is the person first entitled and then to any person in lesser degree of consanguinity. Administration cannot be granted without previously summoning those who have the first natural right, and the same rule applies to Creditors seeking Administration.

For degrees of consanguinity *see* Stephen's Blackstone's Commentaries Vol. 2. ¶ 208.

What Crimes Consuls can deal with.

With reference to Sections 64 to 80—most of which apply to the Supreme Court, it is unnecessary for me to draw attention to any except perhaps the 72nd and then only by warning Consuls not too hastily to determine that the crime of which a person stands

charged before them cannot be adequately punished by the amount of punishment which a Provincial Court has the power to award— namely 12 months imprisonment with hard labour and a fine not exceeding 1,000 Dollars.

Where it is clear on the face of the Depositions taken that the Maximum of punishment for the Offence, if proved, ought not, in the exercise of the discretion which is expressly conferred on Judges and Magistrates by Law, to exceed the amount which a Provincial Court has power to adjuge—then the Consul should proceed to try the case without applying to the Supreme Court.

Imprisonment for any lengthy period, such as a year in China or Japan, is equal to a punishment of three times the same length in England, and the pecuniary loss which is likely to result to any one who has anything to lose is also proportionably greater. The object of punishment is not so much vengeance on the Criminal as to deter others from the commission of similar crimes, and the effect of prompt punishment following on crime to be carried into effect as near to the scene of the commission of the crime as possible is far greater as a deterrent than conviction at a distant place. And to this consideration may also be added the expense incurred either by sending the accused for trial at Shanghai, or that attending the journey of a Judicial Officer of the Supreme Court to the District where the Offence was committed. At the same time there are Offences which when committed in China or Japan require severe punishment, and with this class few considerations founded upon any other basis than that of carrying out in its fulness and entirety the letter of the Law, should enter. *Imprisonment.*

Where under the 77th Section an Assessor dissents from the conviction or amount of punishment awarded, the Consul is bound immediately to send up a full report of the case to the Supreme Court with any reasons that the Assessor may think proper to give for such dissent. *Dissent of Assessor to Conviction.*

Under the 79th Section, the Judge of the Supreme Court is to determine the expediency of sending a convicted offender for imprisonment to Hongkong—Consuls should therefore always state their reasons for desiring that any sentence they pass should be carried into effect within Her Majesty's Dominions—and when desiring that the sentence given by them should be carried into effect at Shanghai or elsewhere in China or Japan they should equally state their reasons. *Sending Convicted Offender to Hongkong.*

The Sections of the Order relating to Treaties and Regulations— unlawful trade with Japan—Japanese waters and piracy—require no comment, any infringement of the three last, as also any Offence under Section 107 committed on board a British Vessel within 100 miles of Coast of China and Japan, must be reported to the Supreme Court at Shanghai. *Treaties and Regulations.*

With reference however to the particular crime of Piracy, it may be remarked that other offences than those of forcibly and feloniously seizing a Vessel on the high Seas are piratical. By Statute some other offences are made piracy: as by Statute 11 and 12 William 3rd Ch. 7 made perpetual by Geo. 1st Ch. 19, if any natural born Subject commits any act of hostility upon the high Seas against others of Her *Piracy.*

Majesty's Subjects under color of a Commission from any Foreign Power; this, though it would be only an act of War in an Alien, shall be construed piracy in a subject. And further (by the same act) any Commander, or other Seafaring person, betraying his trust, and running away with any Ship, boat, ordnance, ammunition, or goods; or yielding them up voluntarily to a pirate or conspiring to do these acts; or any person assaulting the Commander of a Vessel to hinder him from fighting his Ship, or confining him or making or endeavouring to make a revolt on board, shall be adjudged a pirate felon and robber. Again (by the Statute 8 Geo. 1st Ch. 24) made perpetual by 2 Geo. 3rd Ch. 28 the trading with known pirates or furnishing them with stores or ammunition, or fitting out any Vessel for that purpose, or in any wise consulting, combining, confederating or corresponding with them—or the forcibly boarding any Merchant Vessel (though without seizing or carrying her off) and destroying or throwing any of the goods overboard—shall be deemed piracy. Moreover, by Statute 18 Geo. 2nd Ch. 30 any natural born Subject or denizen, who in time of War shall commit hostilities at Sea against any of his fellow Subjects, or shall assist an enemy on that element, is liable to be tried and convicted as a pirate. And, lastly in our own times, a further addition, has been made to the list of piratical offences. For, with the view of putting an effectual stop to the Slave trade, the Statute 5 Geo. 4th Ch. 113 enacts, that if any British Subject, wherever residing, and whether within the Dominion of Great Britain or of any Foreign Country or in the Colonies, shall (except in some particular cases therein specified, within the jurisdiction of the Admiralty) knowingly convey or assist in conveying persons as Slaves or ship them for that purpose, he shall be deemed guilty of piracy, felony, and robbery.

Punishment for Piracy. Formerly the punishment for most piratical offences, was death. But it has been thought expedient to relax this severity and now, whoever shall be convicted of piracy, is liable to be sentenced to penal servitude for life, or any term not less than three years; or to be imprisoned (with or without hard labour) for any term not more than two years. But whoever, with intent to commit or at the time of or immediately before or after committing the Crime of piracy in respect of any Ship or Vessel, shall assault with intent to murder, or stab or wound or unlawfully do any act by which the life of any person on board of or belonging to such Ship or Vessel may be endangered, is liable to suffer death as a felon.

Offences against Religion of Country. It is to be hoped that there will be little occasion to put the stringent powers conferred on Consular Officers by the 100 Section into force, but should it unfortunately be necessary to exercise them —Consuls must remember that the object in view in ordering this class of offences to be dealt with in a summery manner, is the prompt investigation and punishment, if guilty, of the Offender. Immediately a charge is made, or information reaches the Consul that an offence of the kind mentioned in this Section has been committed, he should *immediately* summon the person charged, or if there be good reason to apprehend that he will abscond, cause him to be arrested—and at once enter upon the case giving the accused of course a reasonable opportunity of calling evidence in his own behalf,

and having awarded and enforced the punishment, the whole case should be reported to Shanghai.

It might also be as well for Consuls to have this Section copied out legibly or printed in large type, and to keep it affixed in the most public part of the Consular Office.

The 104 Section gives to the Supreme Court at Hongkong jurisdiction when the accused is actually in the Island of Hongkong, and is there charged with the commission of any crime or offence within a Vessel at a distance of not more than 100 miles from the Coast of China or Japan. When Court at Hongkong has Jurisdiction.

The Section 106 relative to Deportation, requires attention, and Consuls must exercise a sound direction in using the power conferred upon them. Deportation.

While on the one hand it is their duty not only to punish offences on the part of British Subjects but also to prevent breaches of the peace—they must not on the other hand assume too hastily that such and such a course of conduct will result in a breach of the public peace, and there is a distinction to be drawn between conduct which affects or is likely to affect the comfort or security of an individual, and the peace or security of the public—it is only against the latter that this Section is directed—the former is punishable either by fine or imprisonment, or by calling on the offender to find good security for his conduct towards the complainant—and by security is meant not the personal security of the individual complained of, but the security of one or more respectable persons; although this latter security may be dispensed with, as indeed it cannot always in these Countries be found, on the offender depositing with the Consul a sum of money to be forfeited to the Crown on a repetition of the misconduct. Breaches of the Peace.

Continuous Offences however against more than one individual, may be fairly construed into breaches of the *public* peace and are punishable as such—thus if a man is frequently convicted of petty thefts or of attempts at theft—of begging with importunity, or threats —of drunkenness and insulting passers by, or other riotous conduct in the public streets—he may be considered as guilty of committing a breach of the public peace and may be proceeded against under this Section. It is of the utmost importance that what is called in these Countries the "rowdy Class" should be got rid of—and it is this Class who are constantly guilty of conduct towards the Natives— the authorities, and Foreigners, which occasionally is highly criminal, but which generally falls more properly under the head of being subversive of the peace and tranquillity of the public—the Law against Vagrants of all descriptions should be enforced, and thus in time the foreign Settlements will be cleared of persons who are always creating difficulties with the authorities, and who are a source of annoyance and fear to the respectable portion of Foreigners. At the same time in proportion to the extent of the power conferred, will discretion in the exercise of it be required, and any misuse will be regarded in the same light as indifference or neglect. As a general Rule Consular Officers should only act on information given on Oath—the ground of apprehension should be serious and imminent, and if they are then satisfied that there is reason to exercise the Continuous impropriety of Conduct.

large discretionary powers vested in them by this Section, the security demanded should be reasonable. It is also further to be remarked that it is only on failure to give the required security that a British Subject can be deported, except where by the provisions of the Order Deportation is specifically mentioned as a punishment as in Sections 81 and 113.

Registration. Registration under the 114th Section must be seriously insisted no —and after due public notice a Consul should proceed by Summons against those who neglect to comply, in this respect with the Order in Council. On all occasions where a Summons is issued, the expenses of it should be paid by the party summoned—the imposition of a fine is in the discretion of the Consul and should always be imposed when the neglect to register is wilful. It is difficult to carry out the remainder of the penalty as we cannot in justice to the authorities refuse to recognise a British Subject, nor can we often, from mere motives of humanity leave our fellow Subjects—simply because they have not registered themselves—to the tender mercies of the Native authorities. Nevertheless there may be cases when by refusing to recognise in the sense of rendering assistance, Consuls may be able to punish in a most effective manner persons who contumaciously refuse to register themselves.

Registration is eminently a measure of Police and unless Consuls everywhere do their best to make it as a universal as possible, its chief value will be lost.

When a British Subject assumes a Foreign Nationality. When a British Subject has not registered himself in the British Consulate, but has registered himself in a Foreign Consulate—as a Subject of the nationality of that Consulate—the British Consular authority should not recognise him as a British Subject, nor protect him from the consequences of any act done or omitted to be done, or in respect of any liability or responsibility incurred while he was so registered at the Foreign Consulate. Naturalized British Subjects may also be registered but they must produce their letters of Naturalization and it is to be remembered that as against the authorities of the Country of the Birth and Origin of the party naturalized, we cannot protect him from the obligation of being subject to their jurisdiction—except indeed he has been permitted, as is often the case with Prussians, to renounce his allegiance. While on the subject of Registration, I may mention that Foreigners in the employment of British Subjects are not to be registered—nor are they entitled to protection although in some cases where the British Subject is himself injured or inconvenienced in the person of his Servant, an officious assistance may be given to the latter, but never where such Servant has a Consular authority to whom he can appeal.

Foreigners and Foreign Tribunals. With reference to Sub-division XV. "Foreigners and Foreign tribunals" it will be observed that Section 117 is confined to cases in which Foreigners are in the position of Plaintiffs and British Subjects in that of Defendants—the British Consular Court has then jurisdiction, but none can be exercised over Foreigners when in the position of Defendants even if they consent to the case being decided by a British authority. The only way in which effect can be given to a desire on the part of a Foreigner to have any matter of difference between himself and a British Subject decided by

English authority—is by both parties consenting in writing to refer such matters to the arbitrament of the British Consular Officer and in the case of such consent, the assent of the Consular authority of the Foreigner should be also obtained—otherwise in the event of the award being against the Foreigner there is no power which can compel him to perform it. His Consul would no doubt decline on the ground that the proceeding had for its object the withdrawing his Subject from the jurisdiction of his natural authority, and the award would be valueless. Whereas by first asking and obtaining the assent of his Consul—the latter impliedly undertakes to give effect to the award so far as he is able, and there is no objection to requiring such a consent, nor, in the case of a British Subject desiring to submit some difference between himself and a Foreigner to the decision of the Consul of that Foreigner is there any objection to giving it—the submission in the latter case with the consent should be made a Rule of the English Court, and in the event of proceedings against the British Subject becoming necessary they would be based upon the Rule of Court and effect be thus given to the award. (*See Rules* 217 *to* 229.) Reference to Consular Authority by consent.

When reference is made in any of the Sections of the Order in Council (as for instance in Section 119) to the Rules of Procedure —such Rules must be carefully complied with. Reference to Rules of Procedure.

When any appeal is sent to the Supreme Court—the Record must be made up—(*See Rules* 153 *to* 182) and the party appealing must first pay the fees incident to such appeal, and a note of such fees signed by the Consul, must be attached to and form part of the appeal. Appeal.

The Fees on the "motion for leave" on the "security to prosecute the appeal" (which by the bye is only leviable when the security is taken from third persons in the form of a Bond or of a Recognisance, and not as is most usual when the appellant deposits a sum of money to answer the Costs) on the "Order granting the leave" and the "Copying Fees" when any are incurred, belong to the Court from which the appeal issues and must be levied by it and passed to the credit of Her Majesty's Government. What Fees payable, and to what Court.

The Fees on the "Petition" and on the "Hearing" belong to the Supreme Court and must be forwarded contemporaneously with the appeal itself. At the time of sending forward the appeal the Consul should inform the Parties that they are at liberty to appear in person or by Counsel and argue their appeal—or they may put their arguments in writing, and leave the appeal to be decided on the Record and on the written arguments. If they decide to appear in person or by Counsel—notice will be sent to them through the Consul of the day fixed for the hearing—but the Supreme Court will always consult as much as is practicable, the convenience of the parties on their wishes being made known—and should the latter elect to leave the case simply on the Record and the written argument, notice of this election must be given to the Judge of the Court at Shanghai, who will then forthwith and without delay decide the case and send down the judgment in appeal. Except in cases involving points of great importance or when the amount is large, it will be a saving of both time and expense if the case is sent up at once for the Chief

Judge's decision without *viva voce* arguments, and Consulss honld,— without however, exercising any pressure—inform the parties of this.

The Record. The Record should consist of Copies of the Plaint and answer— the notice of trial—the Notes of the Evidence taken by the Consul —with certified Copies of all the documents admitted in Evidence at the Trial—and of the Judgment. And here let me observe that although as a matter of strict right the parties to a suit cannot insist on having a Copy of the notes of the Judge who tried the case for their own use, yet it is highly improper to refuse them when they are wanted for the purposes of an appeal, or for any other really legitimate object. I do not mean to say that a Consul is bound to undergo the labour of copying them himself, or the expense of getting them copied; but he ought to get them copied or let the parties copy them at his option, and if he has a copy made, he may fairly charge the proper fee. It must be recollected that the "Notes" are the only record of the "Evidence" and therefore are of the highest importance—and this fact, coupled with the recollection that a Judge's Notes may become public or may come under the Notice of a Superior Court, should render Consuls very particular in the mode in which such notes are taken by them.

Of what Papers the Record should consist. In addition to the Papers and Documents I have alluded to, there should be a Copy of the Motion for leave to appeal—the Order made thereon—the Petition on appeal and answer, and any arguments which may be filed in support of either. (*See Rule* 170.)

These and a Note of the Fees, constitute the "Record of Appeal." These several documents should be written on the same sized Paper and be fastened together by a piece of Silk or Ribbon to which the Seal of the Court should be affixed—and on the last sheet should be a Certificate of the Consul that the Record so sealed contains true Copies of all the papers in the case. Original documents should not be forwarded—except the case turns upon a question of handwriting, or of identity, or of Erasure, as the Supreme Court cannot assume the responsibility of their safe custody.

Minutes of Proceedings. The 145 Rule orders that in every case, Civil or Criminal heard in the Court, proper minutes of the proceedings should be drawn up and signed by the Judge of the Court before whom they are taken. The Minutes here referred to, are the Orders made by the Court on any application. Thus the order to communicate a Petition or answer is a minute, and so are all orders made on any motion in the case—interlocutory or otherwise—and as a matter of regularity they should be always drawn up and signed.

Proceedings at Trial. The Notes of evidence taken on the hearing of a case, and which consists of the answers of the Witnesses to the questions put by the Parties, must be taken down by the Judge himself in his own Note-Book.

Note-Book. Thus, on the hearing of a case, the Page of the Note-Book should be thus headed:

"1st August, 1866.

C. W. JONES } Plaintiff claims £200 for goods sold and deliver- — Heading of Case.
  v.   } ed.—(See Plaint No. 10.)
J. SMITH.

Defendant says that he has paid the same.—(See answer No. 22.)

(If Counsel appear state their names, &c., &c., and that Mr. * * * opened case for Plaintiff)

Plaintiff sworn—says that, &c., &c.

Cross-examination—

Re-examination—

Under these several headings are to be taken the Notes of Evidence adduced by the Witnesses of the Plaintiff with those of the Cross-examination and Re-examination.

When all the evidence is finished then make a note that such is the

Plaintiff's Case.

Then call on the Defendant who will be entitled to address the Court, but if he intends to give evidence himself he must first be sworn. He is liable like any other Witness to cross-examination and he may after such cross-examination give any explanation he thinks fit of any answer made by him while under cross-examination—this is in fact in the nature of re-examination. The Defendant's witnesses are then called, and the same course pursued as with those called by the Plaintiff. — Examination of Witnesses.

It is a rule that when *either of the Parties* intends to be a witness, he must be sworn—except of course in Criminal cases where the Defendant or rather as he should be called the "accused" is not sworn, neither can he be cross-examined. It is difficult however to see any very good reason for such a prohibition, and probably the next few years will see a change in this respect in our otherwise faultless Procedure, for if an accused person voluntarily tenders himself as a Witness, there is no reason why his evidence should not have the additional guarantee of an Oath—so long as an Oath is supposed to create an additional obligation to speak the truth or why he should not be subjected,—like any other Witness,—to such a test of truth or falsehood as cross-examination offers. — Evidence of Parties. Criminal Cases.

If in the course of the trial any document is referred to and is admitted in evidence—(*See Rule* 248) it should be marked with a "letter" in the Judge's notes of Evidence, and when marked, it forms part of the Record and as such is retained by the Court until the complete termination of the case—all objections made to the admissibility of Evidence should be also taken down in the terms in which they are made, and if, as is very frequently the case, a party is unable to state his objection concisely, he should be requested to put his objection then and there into writing—the other party should reply to the objection, and both the objection and answer should be entered on the notes with the decision of the Court upon the point. (*See the Rules as to Proceedings at the Hearing* 84 to 94.) — Admission of Documentary Evidence.

24

Costs.

The Court should exercise a direction in the matter of awarding Costs—(*See Section* 146 *and Rules* 262 *and* 263) generally speaking —especially where professional Men have not been employed—it will be sufficient to order the party losing the case to pay the Fees—in no case—except where the claim is a fictitious or vexatious one, or the defence an improper one—should the parties themselves be allowed anything for loss of time in attending the Court—nor should Witnesses either be allowed any remuneration, unless before giving their evidence they object to give it until their expenses are paid (*See Section* 148) and then only in the shape of payment for expenses actually incurred, but no such payment should be made if they have come voluntarily and without being summoned. The least that British Subjects in a distant Country, can do, is to assist each other, and when facts are within their knowledge it is not surely too much to expect that they should inform the Court of what they know pertaining to the matter in dispute, gratuitously. If a working man loses however a day's wages or is forced to sacrifice a day's work he may be fairly saved from loss, and so may a professional man; but there is a Class of Witnesses who call themselves "Experts" and these expect a remuneration entirely beyond what they are entitled to. They come merely to express an opinion, and unless they can prove that they actually suffer a pecuniary loss by reason of their obeying the Summons of the Court they should not be allowed anything. Most of these Witnesses have generally made a previous survey of the Ship or goods in dispute, and it has been the custom to pay them very largely for such a service.

Expenses of Witnesses.

Experts Surveys, &c.

The written report of such a survey is inadmissible in evidence, except by consent, and as it was intended for use in Court and paid for, the Fee already charged should always be held to cover the Expenses attending the giving evidence of the result of the survey in Court. Such written surveys may by permission of the Court be referred to, to refresh the memory of the witness.

Consuls will do well however to discourage the expenses attending these surveys, and should particularly discountenance the absurd custom that has grown up in some Ports of making everything, no matter how insignificant or unimportant—a matter of survey— Captains of Vessels seem to think that a survey covers their responsibility, and that protected by such an Act, they can do what they like with the property of their Owners—or that of other people. This is a mistake, a survey leaves their responsibility exactly where it was, and if Captains act improperly, unfairly, or foolishly, they are just as liable whether their act was preceded by a survey or not. On more than one occasion I have had to disregard surveys, and to fix the Captains of Vessels not only with the Expenses of them but also with damages.

When Surveys necessary.

At the same time, Surveys are not unfrequently necessary, as a means—if I may use the expression of perpetuating evidence, when from the nature of the goods, or the circumstances of their arrival —the importance of completing their delivery and the terms under which delivery should be offered or taken,—the goods cannot themselves be produced on the trial of any case having reference to them, in the exact state in which they arrived or were delivered. Surveys

are also of value in matters of Insurance. But a Survey—except by consent of the Parties—never supercedes the necessity of the presence of the Surveyors at the trial and their examination.

I have now exhausted the observations which I have thought it necessary to make on some of the Provisions of the Order in Council. They have been called forth by queries during the past year which have reached me from all sides. I think that a careful perusal of the Order itself would have rendered the answering of many of them unnecessary.

I now pass to the Rules of Procedure confining myself to that portion of them which peculiarly refer to the proceedings before Provincial Consular Courts. Their number has I understand, frightened some Consular Officers who have given up in despair the task of even attempting to understand them—but as from all, conformity to them is imperatively required, and in their own interests as well in that of the general public it is most adviseable, and necessary they should understand and act upon them I will endevour by a running gloss to clear up some of the difficulties to which my attention has been drawn althogh many of them are in reality more imaginary that real. *Rules of Procedure.*

If however the length to which the attempt may oblige me to stretch this Letter is to produce the same results as that produced by the list of Rules, and to secure for it the certainty of not being read, I shall regret the labour employed and the time lost, so much the more, as to the educated Consular Officer, there is the risk of both being considered as most unnecessarily sacrificed.

The object of all Rules of Procedure is simplicity and uniformity, and although many persons may think that these are best obtained by letting people express themselves in their own way—the experience of years has only served to show the utter incapacity of the vast majority of persons to make any ordinary statement in writing of what they really want. Precision of expression and conciseness of language is far more rare than is generally imagined, and the proneness of most persons to indulge in vague declamatory statements generally obscures their meaning to an extent that is hardly conceivable. *Object of Rules.*

It is not Lawyers alone who have felt the value of Forms. The Merchant has recognised it in Bills of Lading, in Bills of Exchange, in Charter-parties and in a great variety of other instruments, and if it had not been for the wise fore-thought and experience which dictated these forms, the amount of litigation would have been infinitely greater than it has been. *Forms.*

In the Rules under consideration in so far as the Petition or Plaint and answer is concerned (*See Rules* 1 *to* 27 *and* 44 *to* 50 *and* 58) there is but one object—namely the development of one or more "issues" that is one or more points of dispute or difference concisely and accurately expressed, and every Judge before proceeding to the hearing of a case should see that the pleadings, in other words, the Petition and answer when read together, disclose an issue. This object is much furthered by adhering to the system of "numbering" the Paragraphs in the Petition and answer—the latter replying specially to those in the Petition either separately or collectively but *Object of Rules. Issues.*

not answering separate parts of two paragraphs in the Petition by one in the answer. Where this cannot be avoided there is probably some defect of clearness in the Petition. Every difference whether it arise out of a disputed question of Law or of fact, can be and therefore must be, concisely stated—and when this is done half the difficulty of decisions vanishes. It is for the purpose of enabling Consuls to frame the real issues in a case, even when the Petition and answer are both defective or wanting in clearness, that such large powers of amendment (*See Rules* 28, 30, 31, 32 *and* 275) have been given—the terms—as to Costs, adjournment, &c., &c., on which these powers should be exercised are in the discretion of the Consular Officer, but he will seldom err, if in their exercise he maintains steadily in view the main object, viz: the developement of one or more simple issues.

Agreement to refer Questions of Fact or Law. There are many cases where both parties could easily agree as to the particular question of fact or Law to be determined between them, and to facilitate the settlement of such questions without formal suit. Sections 1 to 9 inclusive have been framed. The great difficulty is to prevent parties running into a rigmarole statement mingled with reflections and argument.

Very often a forced *viva voce* account of what the one party wants and the other party denies his right to, is an easy mode of getting to the bottom of the subject matter in dispute. With illiterate persons it must generally be resorted to, and the Consul or his Assistant should take down shortly in writing what the Person in the position of Plaintiff claims, and the answer of the Defendant—and having got this down—he may even go a step further and point out that the claim must be supported by evidence and that the answer, if it alleges affirmative matter, must likewise be so supported and notice may then also be given that upon a day to be fixed, each side must come prepared to prove his Statements by the production of evidence. At the same time however, the Consul must guard himself from saying that such or such evidence will be *sufficient*, for while he may point out what is *necessary*, he must not declare beforehand what will satisfy him on the trial of the case, for if he does, each side will either limit himself to the production of such evidence as he supposes the Consul intended, and which in nine cases out of ten will, when produced, be found insufficient or a still worse consequence may be produced by the parties setting themselves to work to fabricate the evidence in support of their cases.

Importance of immediate attention to and decision of Cases. Rules and Forms are however both useless if method, arrangement, and dispatch in business be disregarded, and I cannot too strongly impress upon Consular Officers from the lowest to the highest the importance from a public as well as from a private point of view, of promptness in the dispatch of business. No case should be allowed to linger on the files of the Court. The moment it is brought the initiatory steps should be at once taken, and as soon as possible—subject of course to the Rules of Procedure—it should be brought to a Hearing and a decision. Nothing is so fatal to the interests of a Mercantile Community as delay in the settlement of their differences, and nothing renders the ultimate difficulty of deciding cases greater, than their being allowed to drag on for months unsettled. In the

same way as a good man of business immediately answers a letter the moment it is received, so will an efficient Consular Officer see that no case before him is allowed to linger.

If once the habit of prompt action in all judicial matters is adapted, business becomes easy and the amount of time and labour which it demands, will be found to be comparatively slight.

A great Statesman made it a rule to answer every letter he received the moment he had read it, and no man ever got through an immense correspondence with such extraordinary facility.

A regular system of filing, that is dating and registering every paper the moment it is received, must be adopted, and every Consular Officer should keep a series of Books of uniform size for the different classes of entries he has to make. Thus every Consul must have a Registration Book ruled in the following manner:—

Filing Papers.

Register of Plaints, &c., &c., &c.

Number of Paper.	Date of Registration.	Nature of Contents.	Name of Plaintiff.	Name of Defendant.	Sum sought to be Recovered.	If—when and on whom Served.	Fee charged.

The moment a paper is sent in, it should be read. It should then be numbered and filed, and the Fee that is due on it should be marked. The above columns should then be filled up, and when this has been done the proper order should be endorsed upon it. All papers requiring to be served in a suit must be sent into a Consular Court in Duplicate (*See Rule* 41) One is the original and remains in the Court, the other is a Copy and is served upon the Parties. On the original are endorsed all the above matters which ought to be copied at the foot of the Duplicate and a Certificate under the Consular Seal stating that the Memoranda thus transcribed are true Copies of those on the original petition, should be endorsed on it. Thus for the sake of Example, I will suppose a Plaint is sent into a Consular Court in the following form:—

Registered No. 6, Received 21st August, 1866.

"In Her Britannic Majesty's Consular Court at Chefoo.

"Between James Jones and John Smith, trading as Jones & Co., Plaintiffs,

and

"William Hughes of the Ship "Ann"—Defendant.

"To Her Majesty's Consul

"Sir,

"We beg to present a claim against William Hughes, Master of the Ship "Ann" for stores supplied to him by us at his request. We append the Particulars of our demand* amounting to $500. Although frequently applied to for payment, Mr. Hughes has hitherto neglected to pay.

We therefore request he may be condemned to pay us $500 with $15 for interest from the 1st of January, 1866."

(Signed)   James Jones
                 for Jones & Co."

* Note.—See Rule 28 as to Particulars of demand.

The Party to be served with this Petition is William Hughes, Master of the Ship "Ann" lying at * * *

On this original document the Consular Officer should indorse the particulars which are printed in Red Ink—and at the foot of the Duplicate or Copy which should accompany it—these same particulars are to be written thus:—

Duplicate Petition.

Registered No. 6, Filed 21st August, 1866—Fee $6 ordered to be communicated to the Defendant "William Hughes" of the Ship "Ann" for his answer within 6 days.

I certify the above to be a true copy,

Samuel Williams,
Vice-Consul or Assistant.

Service of Petition.   This Duplicate or Copy is to be served (*See Rule* 42) on and left with the Defendant, (*See Rules* 254 *to* 260) and the Officer serving it will, on his return to the Court sign an endorsement of the fact and the date of the service, which should be written on the Original and copied into the proper Column of the Registration Book.

Margin notes:

Entry of Plaint or Petition and Proceeding thereon.

Fee 1 per cent. $5. Service $1. | $6.

To be communicated to the within named Defendant for his answer within days W. S. in Chefoo, 21st August, 1866.

Served on the Defendant the 22nd August. Charles Smith, Constable.

Service of Petition.

All serving Officers should keep a Book in which they themselves **Service Book to be kept.** should enter a Memorandum of every service effected with the Particulars of it—namely when the document was served, on whom &c., &c., or where left, as this Book will serve to assist their memories when, as is often the case, it becomes necessary to prove in Evidence the fact of the Defendant having been served. For instance this fact must always be proved on Oath, when on the day appointed for the trial the Defendant does not appear—then service must be proved, and when this is done the Plaintiff may proceed to prove his claim and get his verdict. (See Rule 77.)

Great attention should be paid to Rule 38 which has reference to **Parties, Principals and Agents.** the Parties sued, not in the character of Principals, but of Agents for Principals. It is a constant habit here for Plaintiffs to sue people as the Agents of others without seeking to entail any personal liability on the nominal Defendant. Great confusion arises from this practice especially when on Judgment being obtained, and execution applied for, the question arise who is responsible and what is responsible? Had the Agent authority to appear as Agent and defend the suit? who are the Parties on the Record? who is to be the Defendant in the action, if it should hereafter be necessary to put it in suit in Hongkong, India, Australia or England?

The only way of avoiding these points is to follow the Rules.

So also immediately it comes to the knowledge of the Court that **Parties within or out of Jurisdiction of Court.** the Defendant is not within its jurisdiction, it should insist upon evidence that he has been properly served or that substituted service has been allowed, or, if any Person appears for the Defendant, the Court should require such person to produce or file a sufficient authority in writing from the party on whose behalf such person is affecting to act—and in default of evidence of service in the one case or of authority in the other, the Court should refuse to proceed further in the matter.

The same observations apply to answers to Petitions—to Affidavits —to Motions—to Appeals, &c., &c.

The Book in which all Papers are registered will also serve as a **Fee-Book.** check on the Cash Book in which are entered all the Fees received, because the proper Column of it shows the Fee that has been paid on every paper that has been filed. Besides this Book which must always be open to inspection, and of which a transcript may at any moment be required—the Consul must keep his own Judicial Note-Book in which to enter his Notes of the trial of every case as alluded to by me ante P. 22.

He will require also a Book in which to register the Estates of **Registry of Estates of Deceased Persons.** deceased Persons. This Book should be kept in the form of a Ledger —each Estate having a separate Page or rather two separate Pages —on one side of which will be credited to the Estate—with full particulars—all the property received—the amount which, if sold, it realized—in short every particular—and on the other side the Disbursements made on account of the Estate.

Consuls cannot now charge any per-centage on the Estates of deceased persons unless the Supreme Court appoints them Official Administrators. Besides this Book another must be kept in accordance with the form given at Page 93 of the Rules.

In the same way also a Book must be kept of the Estates of Bankrupts in order that it may serve as a check on the Official and Creditors Assignees.

Book of Estates of Bankrupts.

When an answer is sent in to a Plaint, the Consul should see if it contains some distinct averment or denial—if it does—all he has to do is to serve it on the other side, and wait until he receives a request from the Plaintiff that it should be put down for trial. (*See Rules* 60 *to* 80) if such a request is made, he then fixes a day for the hearing according to Rules 60 to 63—but if from a perusal of the Plaint and answer he cannot distinctly understand the issue, or perceive the point in difference between the parties, he would do well to proceed under Rule 58 and summon the parties before him in order distinctly to ascertain the material question in dispute between them—and this—or if more than one—these questions he ought to reduce into writing and they will then supersede the petition and answer, and form the issue or issues to be tried and determined, or he may amend the Petition or answer, either one or both, so as to bring prominently forward the real issues. This proceeding is eminently of an interlocutory character. After the answer no other paper in the form of a reply—ought to be admitted (*See Rule* 56) and if any other appears to be necessary, then it is evident either that the Plaint fails in expressing exactly what the Plaintiff wants, or the answer is deficient in clearness—or sets up some matter which admits the justice of the Plaintiff's claim but shows some reason why he should not be entitled to recover it—such an answer may take the form of a set off under Rule 53 or of a Counter-claim under Rule 55 or without putting in any answer, the Defendant may by motion under Rule 43 pray that the Plaintiff's petition be dismissed inasmuch as even, if true, the Plaintiff would not for some reason or other which he is bound to assign, be entitled to recover upon it. This 43 Rule supplies the place of what in England are called "Demurrers" that is objections in Law to the Plaintiff's obtaining the remedy for which he asks. This is what is called an issue in Law and must be heard and determined in the same way as an issue of fact, with this exception that it is heard on motion, instead of being discussed on the trial of the case. If the Defendant succeeds in convincing the Court that his objection to the Plaintiff's receiving that which he seeks is in Law a good one, the whole case falls to the ground because the only issue between the parties was one of Law and that has been decided against the Plaintiff—the Defendant having rested his defence on that and on nothing else—he has by taking out a motion to dismiss the Petition virtually said "granted that every allegation in the Petition is true, yet I say by reason of the Law being so and so, the Plaintiff is not entitled to recover or he may say that he the Defendant is not in Law answerable." If however the Court is not satisfied that the defence is good in Law, it may under the same Section, order the Defendant to put in an answer in reply to the facts and proceed to the trial of the case on the issues of fact thus joined, and it should always do so when the motion has only been taken out to try the question of legal liability and where it is evident that the Defendant has also an answer on the merits. Whether the issue is one of Law or of Fact the Court should

Answer to a Petition.

Settlement of Issues.

Objections in Law.

decide it on a full and patient hearing, not admitting however of adjournments except the justice of the case evidently demands it (*See Rule* 274) and when able, the presiding Judge should deliver his judgment immediately on the conclusion of the hearing (*See Rules* 95 *to* 98) if however the Consul desires to consider the case, then he may adjourn the delivery of his judgment—giving however due notice when he will be ready to pronounce it. He should then also make some order as to costs, either fixing the amount which the losing side should pay, by naming a fair lump-sum or by decreeing that each party should pay their own costs. On all questions of this kind the Consul should exercise a sound discretion. Judgment.

Rule 99 provides for the giving of any decision subject to a special case, being stated for the opinion of the Supreme Court. This does not mean however that the Consul is to jump to a verdict for either the Plaintiff or Defendant and then leave the whole question of whether he was right or wrong to be decided by the Supreme Court, or that he should suspend his verdict for the opinion of the Supreme Court,—whose verdict it would then be and not the Consul's—but it means that when there arises a distinct question of Law, and sometimes of fact, about which the Consul is doubtful or is unable to make up his mind—he may give a verdict for the Plaintiff or Defendant subject to the decision upon the particular question which the Court above may arrive at. A special case briefly narrating the facts as found in evidence before the Consul must then be sent up, and the question reserved, distinctly stated upon the face of it, and to this question alone will an answer be returned. I have said that it is only "sometimes" on questions of fact that special cases should be stated, because in deciding as to whether the evidence offered proves or disproves a fact, a Consul has the same, if not better means of judging, than the Supreme Court, and it is an important part of his duty to make up his mind on such a subject. Decision subject to a Special Case.

If the parties are not satisfied with his decision they can appeal (*See Rules* 163 *to* 174) and on appeal, the Supreme Court can decide whether or not the Judge below has correctly appreciated the facts before him and given to each due and proper weight and value. In pronouncing judgment it is competent for the Consular Officer to fix a time within which the Defendant is to comply with it, and this course in general prevents delay (*See Rule* 109). Appeal.

On the judgment being given a minute of it should be made in the Judge's Note-Book. Upon this minute—the Decree or Orders is drawn up (*See Rules* 105 *to* 115) and these should be headed with the name of the case thus: Orders on Judgment.

In Her Majesty's Consular Court at * * *
the 30th August, 1866.
John James—Plaintiff.
Between
Edward Edwards—Defendant.
Form of Order.

On the hearing of this Suit it was this day decreed that the Defendant do pay to the Plaintiff the sum $500 with $25 costs of Suit.

| Seal of Court. |

See Rules 105 *to* 115.

Proceedings after Service of Order.

Execution against Goods.

Judgment Summons.

If after a Copy of this Decree has been served on the person required to obey it and he does not comply with it, two courses are open to the party in whose favour it has been made—he may either apply to the Court for execution against the goods of the disobedient party (*See Rules* 116 *to* 128) or he may take out what is called a judgment Summons (*See Rules* 129 *to* 136) that is a Summons which issues on a non-satisfied judgment for the purpose of bringing the Defendant again before the Court in order that he may be examined on Oath as to his means or ability of satisfying or obeying it, and as to the circumstances under which the debt was incurred—and on the hearing of this Summons he may be forced to make a full disclosure of his Estate and property, and in the event of his not having any, should it appear that he has been guilty of the conduct mentioned in Rule 131—he may be imprisoned, and after being discharged, he may again be brought up if the judgment is still unsatisfied, and be again committed, provided it appears that having the means he still refuses to satisfy it, or that he has since his last committement wilfully disabled himself from complying with it (*See Rule* 134) but he will not be liable to be imprisoned a second time, for any cause connected with the matter for which the debt was incurred. If the Judgment Debtor when summoned to appear does not present himself, a Warrant may be issued for his arrest and he may be imprisoned for a short time, for not obeying the Summons.

When to Issue.

Generally speaking, execution against the goods, or a Judgment Summons, or a Warrant of arrest, under Rules 138 and 139 should not issue until the time limited for appealing has elapsed (*See Rules* 154 *to* 162) but there may be circumstances when it may be necessary to order execution of the judgment more or less quickly after service of the decree or Order. The party against whom it is made is then left to apply for leave to appeal, which, if he obtains it, acts as a suspension of all other process, but the Court may under Rule 155 either direct the decision appealed from to be carried into execution, or it may exact security as the price of its ordering its suspension.

Consular Officers cannot well refuse to grant execution on goods on unsatisfied judgments, and it is therefore advisable that in decreeing a time, within which their judgment is to be obeyed, they take into their consideration the position and conduct of the party against whom it is to be enforced. Many actions are the offspring of spite and jealousy—often designedly postponed until a time when the person against whom they are brought is least able to satisfy them—and again many actions are defended that never ought to be defended, and just claims are purposely unsatisfied until the party has lost or made away with all the means of satisfying them.

These are all matters for a Consul in his judicial capacity carefully to consider and he has, generally speaking, from his knowledge of the position and character of his fellow-countrymen ample means and opportunities of information on all such points, and he can always largely avail himself of Rule 113 which enables him to direct the satisfaction of any decree ordering the payment of money by such Instalments as he thinks fit.

An honest man may be ruined by an unjustly hasty execution, when if time were given him he could satisfy the debt—on the

other hand it is to be borne in mind that an indefinite postponement of an Order to pay, may enable a dishonest man to seriously injure his Creditor.

An arrest of the "Person" is a far more serious matter—it is abolished for *debt*—under £20 and when the debt exceeds that sum it should not be hastily resorted to unless the debtor be guilty of the Offences mentioned in Rule 131. There may however be flagrant cases in which the plaintiff should be at liberty to arrest his debtor, leaving him to obtain his release in accordance with the provisions of the Bankrupt Acts. And under Rule 138 when money is not in question, a Warrant of arrest may issue, the effect of which may be to keep a man in Prison for a long period. Personal Arrest.

In some cases it may be expedient and even necessary to refer a case to the decision of one or more persons. Reference of Questions of Account.

Questions of Account may at any time after the commencement of a Suit be referred, and the Judge has power, even without the consent of either party, to order the Accounts to be taken by some qualified person (*See Rule* 58). Of course it is always desirable to get the parties to agree to name some one, in whom they both have confidence, and when this is done care should be taken to fix the fee or remuneration which the Referee will be entitled to, otherwise difficulties and objections are apt to arise at the last moment. When a Referee can be induced to take the case as a friend to both parties and without fee, this should always be preferred. When it cannot be done, the Consul should fix a reasonable sum, but it must be borne in mind, that a Referee cannot be compelled to accept a reference.

In the course of a Suit however there may be many interlocutory proceedings (*See Sub-division VI of Rules*) to which it may be well now to refer. It is in these proceedings that I have found most irregularity to prevail. People are inclined to think that they are of very little importance, that there is no necessity to keep a record of them, and that they are beside the real merits of the case. No mistake can be greater. There ought to be the same regularity in granting or refusing a Motion, as in deciding the case itself, as both the grant or the refusal may seriously affect the ultimate decision. The object of most, if not all interlocutory Proceedings, is to remedy some error in the original proceedings or to get relief of some kind or another—such as to hasten or delay some stage in the trial of a cause—or to force one party to do some act which the justice of the case requires—such as to find security for Costs—or not to leave the jurisdiction of the Court, or to amend or consent to the amending of some of the proceedings. Interlocutory Proceedings.

The mode in which such applications are to be made is very clearly explained in *Rules* 144 *to* 152—and the widest discretion is given to Judicial Officers as to the allowing, varying or refusing them. As a general Rule no Order on an interlocutory application, which affects or may affect the interests or position of the other side in a case, should be definitively made until an opportunity has been afforded to such other side to object to it. The best course is to summon the other party to appear on a certain day and show cause why the Order prayed for should not be granted. This gives an opportunity to the other side to read the Affidavits upon which the Motions to show Cause.

application is based—to prepare others by way of answer to them, and to consider the objections to the Order as asked. Care should always be taken that statements of fact made in support or in opposition to the application, if they are of such a nature as to influence the Court in granting or in refusing it, should be made on Oath, and in the form of an Affidavit (*See* 4th *Paragraph of Rule* 145 *and Rules* 149, 151 *and see Rules as to Affidavits* 230 *to* 242). As a rule if the parties have appeared by Counsel, Costs should on these interlocutory proceedings be given to the side that gets the decision on the application in his favour, but where the resistance to the Order prayed for was reasonable, the Court may even if it grants the Order, refuse to allow Costs and thus leave each party to pay their own, or if it thinks the propriety or impropriety of the application can only be ascertained by the ultimate decision in the cause, the Costs may be left to be costs in the cause, in other words to be paid by the party against whom the verdict is pronounced. When a party desires to make a motion he should be told to make it in writing in accordance with Form 8 annexed to the Rules and having paid the Fee and filed his Affidavits—if any—(of which Office Copies must be left or made) in the Office of the Court, the Consul should consider whether the application is one that he can grant without injury to the other side. If he thinks he can, he may do so, but if as I have already said he thinks the application is one that may possibly affect the other side, he should merely grant an Order calling on the other side to show cause against it on a certain day—and if no cause is shown, then he may grant it, but an appeal will lie from the Court below to the Supreme Court in all cases where the Order appealed from has not been made *ex-parte*—that is—on the simple application of one party only (*See Rule* 153).

Motions.
In hearing Motions Consuls should pursue the same course as on hearing causes—they should take Notes in their Note-Books heading the Motion as of the cause—state who appeared—refer to the affidavits by the registered numbers—and shortly state the arguments offered on both sides and then conclude by a Note of the decision. The mode in which the Record of an appeal from a decision on a Motion is made up is stated in Rule 176 and Rules 175 to 178 regulate the Proceedings.

Questions of Law or Fact.
In actual practice there will be found many cases in which both parties can, as I have before mentioned, if it is suggested to them, easily agree upon the particular question of Law or of Fact in difference between them, and to facilitate the settlement of such questions, Rules 1 to 9 were specially framed. All that the Parties have to do is to consent to leave such and such questions to be determined by the Consul. The questions must of course be reduced to writing—the Consul is then to summon the parties before him and having satisfied himself that the question or questions is or are not idle, but that they have a direct interest in their determination, may make an order in which he embodies the question as in Form 1 and the case proceeds as at an ordinary hearing—if it is a question of Law, the Consul can hear such legal arguments as the parties think proper to offer in support of their respective positions—if a question of fact—then he will have to hear the evidence which both

sides may bring to support the statement that either of them has made. The Fees on such cases must be calculated on the same basis as if the case was tried in the usual way—and the mode of taking Notes—delivering judgment, &c., &c., are identical.

In the grant of Summary Orders before suit (*See Rules* 179 to 182) the greatest precaution is absolutely necessary. Summary Orders before Suit.

Nothing but "extreme urgency" will justify a Consul acting under this Rule and he should carefully see that the immediately following Rules are complied with.

The remainder of the Rules are so clear that it is unnecessary for me to enter into any more explicit explanation. The best way of recollecting them that I can suggest is for the Consular Officer to refer to them for his guidance whenever he is called upon to do anything about which they treat. If this is done, a dozen of such references will soon impress them on the memory and render unnecessary constant reference, except in particular cases. Thus when an affidavit is tendered to a Consul, he should at once turn to Rules 230 to 242 and having carefully read them through, see that the affidavit before him complies with the essential requisites. So with reference to arbitration—the course to be pursued under the head of Probate and Administration—and indeed under all other subdivisions.—The Consular Officer must endeavour to recollect, and if he cannot recollect, he must take the trouble to refer to the Index to see if any and what provisions are applicable to any particular case or circumstances that may be before him. Importance of constant reference to Rules of Procedure.

On many occasions I have had to send back cases, and in many cases to dismiss them, simply because the Rules as to Attorneys and Agents—Proceedings against Partnerships or where the Plaintiff was out of the jurisdiction,—service, &c., &c., &c., had not been complied with. In almost every instance the Consular Officer stated that he had no knowledge of the Rule—the non-observance of which had entailed loss, expense and delay to the Parties. Yet the Rule existed, but had not been referred to. While I am now writing—an affidavit is put into my hands having come down from a British Consulate. It appears to have been sworn before two Consuls at different Consulates—but whether by one Deponent before two Consuls—or by two Deponents—each deposing before the Consul of the district within which at the time of swearing he happened to be—or which Consul swore which Deponent—is on the face of the document a profound mystery. If a reference had been made to the Rules this complication of difficulties would have been avoided.

It appears unfair to presume that neither Order in Council or Rules of Procedure have been read—yet not to presume it in many instances would lead to the less complimentary conclusion that if read, they had not been understood.

In addition to the Rules framed by myself under the power specially conferred by the Order in Council there are others framed by Her Majesty's Minister at Peking to which Consular Officers must pay attention. The first of those recently published is for the Registration of Mortgages—the second for the Registration of Bills of Sale, and the third enables parties to sue the Agents of quasi Companies or Co-partnerships in those cases where the individual Rules framed by H. M.'s Ministers at Pekin or Yeddo.
Registration of Mortgages.
Bills of Sale.
Suits against Partnerships and Agents.

Members or Co-partners of such bodies are not known. This Regulation is an important one and should be carefully read over by all Her Majesty's Judicial Officers in China and Japan, as it not only alters Rule 252 very materially, but at any moment Consuls may be called on to give course to suit commenced against the Agents or one of the Partners of any one of the numerous unincorporated Companies which exist in both these Countries, and unless this new Regulation is carefully attended to and acted on, great delay and loss may be the result in the judicial settlement of this class of cases. It is needless to observe that the Agent or Member of such Co-partnerships so sued must be a British Subject, otherwise no British Consular Court can exercise any jurisdiction over him.

Importance of Reference to Levant Circular Letter.

A variety of Miscellaneous information as to the conduct of judicial business will be found in the Extract from the Circular Letter addressed to the Levant Consuls and reference is now particularly made to that portion of it which treats of the different steps in an Action—of Damages,—of Evidence—and of Bankruptcy.

Distress by Landlord.

It may perhaps be as well that I should mention a mode by which a Landlord can obtain his rent other than by an action of Debt, and also a process by which he can recover possession of the premises themselves—neither of these processes are alluded to in the Rules of Procedure, but as they are sometimes resorted to by persons in the position of Landlords, or of Owners of property out here, it may be useful briefly to refer to them. These remedies can of course only be enforced against British Subjects, because where the Tenant or party in possession is a foreigner, recourse must be had to the foreign tribunal. In England a distress for Rent in arrear, can be put in by a Landlord without the intervention of a Court of Justice. Here it is most inexpedient that such a remedy should be resorted to without the knowledge and consent of the Consular Officer, inasmuch as it is a proceeding calculated to cause a breach of the Peace and also because there are no sworn brokers or appraisers of Property. Before such consent should be given the Consul should satisfy himself that a tenancy has been created—that a distinct agreement has been entered into by which a fixed rent at fixed periods has been reserved—that there has been an occupation under such agreement—that rent is in arrear—and unpaid, and that due application has been made for payment of it. The facts should all be clearly stated on Affidavit. A Warrant may then issue under the Consular Seal authorizing the entry on the Premises and the seizure of the goods therein, and after the lapse of five days, the sale of so much of the goods and chattels of the Tenant as may be found in the Premises may be made to satisfy the rent in arrear and the costs of executing the Warrant of distress. Immediately on the entry of the Officer—he should produce and read to the Tenant, or any one in Possession, the Warrant, and if payment of the sum endorsed on it is not tendered, he should proceed to make an Inventory of sufficient goods to satisfy the amount. Some person should then be left in possession, but care should be taken, not to seize more than is absolutely requisite to cover the rent, costs, and Expenses.

Proceedings to Recover Possession of Premises.

To recover possession of Premises, if it is the Landlord who claims he should state in his Petition that the Tenancy has expired either

by notice to quit—effluxion of time or otherwise—and this he must prove on the Trial to entitle him to a delivery of the possession of the Premises—the Petition must state all the facts of the Tenancy, &c., &c., and it must be served on the Tenant or Tenants in possession whether they are sub-Tenants or hold direct from the Petitioner. Any one can come forward and defend the right to the possession, but he, as well as a Tenant or occupier, is liable to be called upon to give security for Costs to be paid to the Petitioner in the event of his —the Defendant's—non-success. At the trial—the Plaintiff must show either that he is the Owner—or that he is in the position of Landlord. A Defendant may dispute his right to the Ownership and show it is in himself or in some else, but he cannot open up any such question if the Petitioner proves that the relation of Landlord and Tenant existed between them—inasmuch as it is a rule of Law, that a Tenant cannot dispute the title of his Landlord. If the Petitioner succeeds in satisfying the Consular Officers that the Occupier is a trespasser having no right, or being a Tenant his right has expired and determined, a judgment may pass for the Petitioner ordering possession of the premises to be given up to him, and under such a judgment, an order may be drawn up, and on this Order the proper Officer of the Court may oust the party in possession and give the same to the Petitioner.

These remedies are not often resorted to out here, nor should they too hastily be permitted. At the same time cases may arise requiring that they be resorted to, and in such cases the Consular Officer is bound to see that they are not abused by irregularity or unnecessary harshness.

For "Distress" *see* Woodfalls' Landlord and Tenant and Stephens' Blackstone 3 Vol. ¶ 356 et seq.—and for "Possession" *see* Common Law Procedure Act, 15 and 16 Vict. Ch. 76, Sec. 210 et seq.

In the same way and with the same formalities as are to be observed in the conduct of Ordinary Civil and Criminal cases, should Consuls conduct Civil or Criminal cases of a summary character under which latter head must be classed the Criminal sections of the Merchant Shipping Act. *Importance of Regularity of Procedure in Summary Cases.*

In the Consul's Note-Book should appear the date of the trial— the names of the Parties—the cause of Action—if a Civil case—or the alleged Offence if a Criminal case—the number of the Summons— the evidence adduced by the parties—and the judgment—so that at any time a reference to the notes will bring the whole case before the mind of any one under whose notice it may at any future time be brought.

No instructions to Consular Officers on the subject of their Judicial duties would be complete without at least reference to that branch of them which arises out of the position in which they stand towards their countrymen to whom has been delegated, or who have assumed, towards and amongst each other the responsibilities, within the different concessions at the Treaty Ports of China and Japan, of a system of self-government. *Consuls, and Municipal Councils, &c., &c., &c.*

Whether this Government, so far as it extends, is carried on by a Municipality or by a Committe of Land-renters, the Consul will always be called on to play an active part in reference to it, because in him alone resides all coercive authority. No taxation can be compelled without his decree. No Police regulation enforced except by his Order.

Now the source of the Authority of Consuls in the matter of these *quasi* local Governments, and of these self-governing powers themselves, is almost the same. They both spring from the Powers which it has pleased Her Majesty to give to her Diplomatic Representatives in China and Japan for the preservation of peace, order and good government amongst Her Subjects residing in or resorting to those Countries. Therefore all Rules and Regulations which have these ends in view, and which are framed and promulgated by the Representative of the Crown are binding on British Subjects. The Machinery which is employed to bring them into action may be different, but the Motive power is the same. In one place the Minister may delegate his powers within certain limits to a Committee of Land-renters—to the elected of Tax or Rate payers—or to any other body. In another place, he may confer it on the Consul alone—but inasmuch as in almost every case funds would be required to carry out the most ordinary measures of public advantage and utility, it is not likely that the task of levying or administering such funds would be thrown on the Consular Officer—and there would be besides grave constitutional difficulties in the way of such a proceeding. It may therefore be assumed that wherever there is a sufficiently large Community, the task of providing for their wants as a social body will be left to the Community themselves, but always in consequence and by virtue of some regulation to that effect emanating from the Chief Diplomatic Authority: while, as I have before said, the task of giving an executive or compulsory effect to such measures as the Community may determine amongst themselves in the interests of the public to be necessary, will be left to the Consul. It is therefore to these Regulations the Consul must look before he exercises the authority vested in him, to see if what he is asked to do, is within the limits of the delegated powers conferred on those who ask him to enforce any rule made by them. Within such limits he may safely act and enforce action, beyond, his own power as well as theirs, is absolutely nil. A Consul of his own motion has no power to impose a Tax or a Rate or a Due,—he cannot make a Port-regulation or license a public House or a place of amusement—neither can he (except at his own Expense) build a road, or enforce sanitary regulations.

But Her Majesty's Minister may enable a Community to tax themselves for all these purposes, and make regulations to the same effect, and he may also give an authority to the Consul to enforce regulations so made, provided that what is done, is done and is necessary to be done for the peace, good order and government of British Subjects residing in or resorting to China and Japan. At the same time there are Offences against good order, which although generally breaches of special Municipal regulations are also not unfrequently breaches either of the Common Law or of the general Statute Law of England, and these may be punished under the general Magisterial powers, possessed by Consuls. Thus for instance, it may not, in the absence of a special Municipal regulation,

be an Offence to have a Dung Heap or a Deep hole outside a man's door, but if a direct injury to an individual results therefrom and can be proved, the party injured has a remedy by action—so also quick driving through a settlement may not be an offence *per se* when no Municipal Regulation has made it one, but if any one is injured by such driving, such injury is a fair ground of complaint and is punishable—if wilfully done—by the Criminal Law, and if not so wilfully done by an action for damages.

As I intimated at the beginning of this letter, most of the observations and explanations I have offered on the Order in Council and Rules of Procedure, have been called forth by queries actually addressed to me during the past year, and to which I have from time to time replied. I take this opportunity of making these replies generally known, and I trust, whether considered pertinent or necessary by all H. M.'s Consular Officers, they will be received in the spirit in which they are made—namely to assist all in the carrying out of a system established and devised for the general benefit.

Yours &c.,

EDMUND HORNBY.

Extract from General Instructions to Her Majesty's Consuls in the Levant by the Judge of the Supreme Court, revised and rendered applicable to H. M.'s Consuls in China and Japan.

SUPREME COURT.

THE Provincial Courts must look to the present Order in Council and the Rules as wholly containing within themselves the codes (so to speak) of law and of procedure which they are to administer. Where the Order and Rules contain no express and specific provision on any point of law or of procedure, there the law and practice of England must be followed, so far as is practicable, and subject also to the continuance of any convenient practice of a Consular Court which is not in conflict with any part of the system established by the present Order and Rules.

I need scarcely, however, point out that my remarks are only in the nature of comment and elucidation, that the Order in Council and Rules form the Consular Officer's authoritative guide, and that it is his duty to study and make himself thoroughly master of their contents.

Jurisdiction of Consular Court.

The relations of the Consular Courts in the different Treaty Ports of China and Japan to the Supreme Court are defined with exactness in the Order and Rules, and the mode in which appeals to the Supreme Court are to be prosecuted is precisely laid down. It seems to me unnecessary therefore to dwell on this part of the system, however important, and although to a considerable extent remodelled. I will content myself with drawing special attention to the fact, that while the jurisdiction of a Consular Court at the Ports is in most respects complete in cases coming within the scope of its authority and arising within its own local jurisdiction, yet the Supreme Court is in all cases invested with a concurrent jurisdiction, so that where the circumstances render it desirable, any case may be originally and in the first instance heard and determined by the Supreme Court wherever it may arise, in China or Japan.

This general jurisdiction of the Supreme Court may be exercised either at Shanghai or on the occasion of the Chief Judge or a legal officer of the Supreme Court visiting, in a judicial or magisterial capacity, a Consular Court in the Provinces. Such visits may be compared in some respects to the circuits of the Judges of the Superior Courts in England.

It will probably be in most cases convenient that civil suits heard by the Supreme Court under this branch of its authority should be brought up to Shanghai, but that criminal prosecutions should be disposed of on the spot, especially where the witnesses are numerous, or the case is a grave one and a local example of punishment is required.

It will be the duty of the Provincial Courts, including the Supreme Court, to reciprocally assist in carrying on the due administration of justice under the Order in Council and Rules, by executing one another's decrees and orders, taking examinations of witnesses, serving summonses and petitions for one another, and, in short, in every way facilitating to the best of their ability, and according to the exigency of the case, the prosecution of a suit or proceeding, civil or criminal, pending in any part of China or Japan.

Reconciliation.

The obligation of promoting the reconciliation of persons between whom differences may arise is expressly laid on the Courts by the Order in Council. The duty is one which ought to be discharged with firmness, but at the same time with tact and discrimination.

Every encouragement and facility should also be given by the Court to arbitrations.

And where the questions in dispute are simple and clear, the parties should be advised or directed to have recourse to the modes prescribed at the beginning of the Rules for obtaining the decision of questions without the formalities of a suit. In this way controversies on matters of fact may be readily and advantageously disposed of by any Provincial Court, while the parties can with ease obtain the opinion of the Supreme Court on any point of law which may be involved in the controversy between them.

There will, however, necessarily be a large proportion of cases in which, for a variety of reasons, no determination can be come to without regular proceedings in Court. I shall now turn to the consideration of this class of cases.

The great bulk of judicial business must always consist of what are known as civil suits, that is, cases where one party claims either a debt or damages from another, or seeks to have his adversary ordered by the competent authority to do, or to abstain from doing, some particular thing. It will be proper to consider this large branch of judicial business in the first place, and apart from such special branches as bankruptcy, the administration of intestates' property, &c., because not only is it the most common of all the methods of legal proceeding, but moreover it involves the principles which permeate every branch of the law as administered in England. So that a person who has a knowledge of the true principles on which the English procedure in civil suits is based, finds no difficulty in bringing that knowledge to bear on any special branch of law which he may unexpectedly be called on to administer, and is consequently enabled to master these particular branches, in cases where difficulties arise from a want of special direction, by a recurrence to the general and first principles from which all rules are supposed to be derived. I propose, then, first to speak of the principles of procedure in civil cases, using all these words in the widest sense. Of what Judicial Business chiefly consists.

A civil case or suit between parties may be considered as a reference by one to the civil authority of a claim which he asserts against the other, and it is a reference which the adversary is obliged to accept. By whatever form of process such a proceeding is begun, the plaintiff's object ought to be to show, that under a certain state of facts which has arisen, he has a right in law to demand that a certain order be made by the civil authority, whether calling on the defendant to pay money to the plaintiff as a debt, or as a compensation, or as damages; or, in a certain class of cases, where the principles of law recognize a right of interference, calling on the defendant to do, or to abstain from doing, some particular act. The essential points are, that on such and such facts (which the plaintiff, if they shall not be admitted, must be ready in due time to prove, so far as they are necessary to support the right), he, the plaintiff, has a right in law, to a certain judicial order on the defendant.

Special provisions are made by the Rules for summary procedure in cases where the plaintiff claims less than 100 dollars (*Rules* 10 *to* 12), and for the administration of the property of deceased persons (*Rules* 13 *to* 17); but although these provisions are calculated to be of very extensive and beneficial application, I think the observations which I am about to make on the more formal proceedings originated by petition will be sufficiently explanatory of these summary provisions also. Summary Procedure.

The summary procedure on bills of exchange, &c. (*Rules* 18 *to* 25), it is to be noted, is applicable in all cases where proceedings are instituted within six months after the bill or other instrument becomes due and payable, without any limitation with respect to the amount for which the bill or other instrument is drawn.

These provisions are of great importance as affording an extremely rapid and simple process for the enforcement of mercantile obligations.

The ordinary form of commencing a suit is by a petition. This Petition.

has hitherto often been in the shape of a letter to the Consular authority; and although a more formal document, such as is indicated in the Rules, is desirable, and ought to be required by the Court, wherever possible, yet it is not intended that a person applying to the Court for relief should be absolutely precluded from communicating by a mere letter, for there are many men who can state a ground of claim, and express the relief they seek, and assert their title to it, in this familiar form, who would be quite puzzled to draw anything which resembled a declaration, or a short claim or bill in Chancery.

In matter of form, the only thing which appears absolutely requisite is, that the name of the party sued should be placed conspicuously on the paper; and the relief desired be distinctly asked for, so that a defendant may know what is sought from him, and the Court may know what it is asked to do: but under whatever form clothed, these essential particulars must be contained in the petition, and if it falls short in this respect, it is either defective or altogether and radically bad. It is defective, where the facts are contained only inferentially, or in such a manner as not to enable the defendant to lay his hand on each separate material fact, and say, "I admit this," or, "I deny this;" the facts to support the legal right must be, and must be stated to be, actual facts: it is defective, if certain facts really existing and necessary to support the claim or right, are omitted and passed over, which continually arises from the ignorance and want of care of the person making the claim: it is defective, where the relief demanded is not properly demanded, although the facts stated, if proved, would give a right to some other relief: it is defective again, where the facts are not stated with such particularity as to give the defendant sufficient notice of the nature of the claim made against him, and of the transactions in respect of which it is made. On the other hand the claim is bad, either when it is made against a wrong person altogether, or when all the material facts are fully stated, and on all the facts there does not actually exist, as a legal consequence thereof, the right to the relief asked, or to any relief capable of being granted under the petition.

Division of Defective and bad Claims.

It appears to me that this division into defective and bad claims is one which is convenient to be observed and acted on in places where competent professional assistance is most difficult, if not impossible to be obtained; and the result of an objection to the petition or claim ought to depend in a great measure on the question, to which of the two classes any claim open to objection should be referred.

It is obvious, that if the "claim," "petition," "letter" (by whatever name, in short, it may be called), is "bad," in the sense in which I have used that word, then it must fail altogether, no amendment being possible, and it must fail at any period of the suit at which its "badness" is brought to the knowledge of the Court. It is the defendant's duty, and it would generally be his interest to bring this badness to the notice of the Court at the very earliest period. This, in English practice, is done by what is technically called "demurring," and is founded on a supposed admission of

the absolute truth of all the facts alleged in the pleading demurred to; the party demurring contending only, that on these facts as appearing on the face of the pleading the claimant has not the right in law which he claims. The result in English practice of a failure in sustaining this exception is sometimes final judgment, the party not being permitted to dispute the facts once admitted; in other cases, he is allowed to have admitted the truth of the facts only for the purpose of his argument, and on his demurrer being overruled, is at liberty to answer or plead, denying all or any of the facts. In the Consular Courts, I am of opinion that the most convenient course is that which the Rules lay down (*Rule* 43), namely, that the defendant is to be taken as admitting the truth of the allegations of the petition only for the purpose of argument, and that with the leave of the Court he may afterwards controvert those allegations by his answer, if his motion to dismiss the petition on grounds of law fails. If the claim or petition is not bad, but only defective, then the result of the discovery of the defect, when brought to the notice of the Court, either at or before the hearing, ought to be that the plaintiff must remedy the defect, and pay the costs to which his carelessness, neglect, or ignorance has put the defendant, as well as the costs of any necessary adjournment for the purpose of amending; but it is the defendant's duty, in cases where the claim is defective by reason of some uncertainty, or want of information sufficient to enable him to answer, to bring the matter forthwith before the Court to have the claim made more precise and full; and where a defendant fails in doing this, either from neglect or ignorance, or to ensure further delay, when the defect in the claim does become manifest at the hearing, he must not expect to recover costs from the plaintiff for an injury, the remedy for which he had in his hands and has neglected to use.

It is proper to say a word or two on the irrevelant, and often personally abusive matter with which petitions and answers are filled. I think it desirable to discourage lengthy pleadings, and a constant interchange of them in the same suit. It is obviously proper to force parties to omit offensive imputations foreign to the subject, and not to put in mere abuse, under any circumstances. The length of written pleadings here, and their number, were under the old system enormous, and in many cases it would have been difficult for any human being to ascertain from some of the later papers in a cause, what was the subject of the original suit; the cause was delayed, the parties irritated, and the expenses increased beyond all bounds by this constant interchange of documents, which for the most part raised either no issue or only immaterial and collateral ones, and the Court had at last, with labour and difficulty, and without any corresponding certainty of achieving success, to fish out from this mass of matter the real question or questions in dispute. Answers.

The claim of the plaintiff must, of course, be communicated to the defendant, and as a general rule this must be done before any step whatever is taken by the Court in relation to it, but there are certain exceptional cases known to the English law, and familiar to the practice of the Consular Courts, in which the Court, on the applica- Special Applications to Suits.

tion of the plaintiff, and for the purpose either of preventing irremediable mischief, or more generally of securing its own efficacious jurisdiction over the party sued, or some particular property in dispute, interferes by an order affecting the interest of the defendant, and made in his absence.

Orders to hold to Bail. Sequesters. Detention of Ships. Of such cases are orders to hold to bail; orders of sequester on property; and orders to detain ships; and also a class of orders in the nature of *ex parte* injunctions in the English Chancery practice.

If I may judge by the experience of Consular Courts, and from the information I have sought for and obtained, applications of this description are amongst the most common, and, at the same time, there is often no more delicate task that can be imposed upon a Judge than the granting or refusal of such an order. The very peculiar circumstances under which British subjects reside here, and the nature of their mercantile pursuits, which often makes it necessary for them to leave one place for another at a short notice, even when they have every intention of returning, render it easy to supply so much of the material for an application to hold to bail as consists in the intention of the defendant to leave the jurisdiction, while the consequences of a legal detention are frequently serious to mercantile enterprise, and must be always detrimental to the credit of the party. There is no one thing that a mercantile man has a greater aversion to than to ask another to be his bail; nor is it always easy, at a very short notice, to pay money into Court. Again, the consequences of sequestrations granted on property are too often serious in the extreme,—loss of credit, loss of markets, loss of custom, especially from foreign merchants, who only know that they are disappointed in the promised delivery of goods which they had a right to expect. But if it should be said that these evils are sometimes inseparable from the general use of a just and beneficial remedy, I must remark that not only do the exceptional circumstances of trade in China and Japan make the proper use of this particular remedy more difficult, and the concomitant evils much more frequent and severe, but also here at least, it is sought to be used as a method of pressure for forcing some settlement of justly disputable claims, to a degree which makes the greatest care and caution necessary on the part of every judicial officer in dealing with applications of this nature.

Evidence necessary to hold to Bail. The evidence to support the application must be the same as on an application to hold to bail, which I shall now proceed to consider.

Before granting an order to arrest and hold to bail in a civil suit the Court must be satisfied that there is a debt of 20*l*. or its equivalent in dollars or upwards owing to the plaintiff, and then payable from the person against whom the application is made; or that the plaintiff has a cause of suit against the defendant to the amount of 20*l*. or upwards, or has sustained damage to that amount, and that there is probable cause for believing that the debtor or defendant, unless he be forthwith apprehended, is about to quit the jurisdiction, with intent to avoid or delay the plaintiff, or with intent to remain out of the jurisdiction so long that thereby the plaintiff will or may be delayed in the recovery of the debt or damages. Also, a suit must have been already commenced (*See Rules*

179 *to* 182 *and see Rule* 261), except, in those cases of extreme urgency where the Court thinks itself justified in taking the plaintiff's formal undertaking to begin a suit within a certain definite number of hours or days. It is obvious that no judicial officer ought to be satisfied of these particulars except on the oath, or affirmation where allowed by law, of one or more person or persons; and it is the practice in England, and must not be relaxed here, to require affidavits, that is, written statements on oath (or affirmation where allowed by law), wherein the debt is positively sworn to as then payable by the party against whom the application is made, or containing positive statements of facts by which the Judge is satisfied that the plaintiff has a cause of action against the defendant to the amount of 20*l*. or upwards; and the affidavit should not only contain a statement of the positive belief of the deponent as to the approaching departure from the jurisdiction of the defendant, and of his intention thereby to delay, or its probable effect in delaying the recovery of the debt, or the other remedy on a judgment, but it should contain a statement of the facts on which that belief has been formed and is founded, for it is the Court that is to be satisfied. And where the facts are acquired at second hand, either an affidavit of the informant should be obtained, or a reason given why that has not been done, and the name of the informant, and time, place, and circumstance of the information, should be supplied.

With reference to the meaning that should be attached to the words "out of the jurisdiction," in practice I am inclined to lay down that they should generally be construed with reference to the intention of the defendant, to go and remain for some substantial time altogether out of the jurisdiction of the Consular tribunals in China or Japan: but in this matter, where customary procedure ought to go for much, I am desirous to leave a discretion to the several Consuls. It would be hard to prevent a man who was living at Ningpo or Chefoo, but whose affairs might call him imperatively to proceed to Shanghai, and remain there for some prolonged period, from doing so without finding bail to an action which might be prosecuted as effectually and readily in his absence, if he left after service of the petition, more especially as it will henceforth be the duty, as it has been heretofore I understand the practice of every Provincial Court to execute the judgments of the Courts of other districts. On the other hand, to allow a debtor to remove from Shanghai to Calcutta, would be often attended with the greatest possible risk of losing that security which control over the person of the debtor is supposed to afford. <small>Meaning of term "Out of Jurisdiction."</small>

On the whole, I repeat that this point ought to be left to the discretion of the several Consuls, whose duty it is to hold an even scale between the parties, and leave all reasonable freedom of action to the debtor which is not inconsistent with reasonable security to the creditor.

The Judges in England will not readily hold to bail except on a distinct affidavit of debt, or of damages capable of being then ascertained; therefore no claim for mere damages, altogether unliquidated, ought, as a general rule, to support such an application. <small>Damages ought to be "Liquidated."</small>

When the application is made by a foreign subject, even still more <small>Foreigners applying.</small>

caution is necessary, for from the fact of the foreign nationality, one great check on reckless assertion is withdrawn. I apprehend that it would be a difficult task to procure the certain and adequate punishment of a foreign subject detected in perjury in such a case; at all events, I am sure the fear of such punishment would not be present to the mind, so that increased care, before acting, is the only safeguard.

Finally, it is to be borne in mind, that it is in the discretion of the Consul to refuse the Order, even although he be satisfied that the defendant is about to depart the jurisdiction; but if he is satisfied of the intention or effect of the proposed departure, and of the claim in debt or damages, he ought to grant it.

The practice of issuing sequesters on the application of the plaintiff is not unusual, and appears rather to have been borrowed from the foreign codes than to be derived from any analogous English procedure. The remedy is in some cases strictly analogous to one known in the city of London as "foreign attachment;" as where the money belonging to a debtor is attached or sequestered in the hands of a third party.

This ought never to be permitted, except on a distinct positive affidavit of debt payable at the time of making the application by the party whose money is sought to be attached; and the case ought to be made out *primâ facie* to the satisfaction of the Court before such an attachment is allowed. In other instances, with regard to goods, the habit is to procure the legal enforcement by sequester of a right of "stoppage *in transitu;*" the consignor obtaining an order of the competent Court on the person in whose hands the goods are, to hold them until the right to stop them has been adjudicated upon. This seems strange at first sight, because in theory in such cases the person holding the goods must be taken to be the agent of the consignor, but in practice it is, I believe, convenient, and the custom is general.

A great number of applications for sequesters would in England be made in the Court of Chancery for injunctions, and it is proper to observe that extreme caution is necessary before granting them at all. It appears to be looked on here by many persons, especially foreigners, almost as a matter of course that the Court should, in case of any dispute about the terms or performance of a mercantile contract, instantly, and by way of commencement of the proceedings, lay an embargo on any of the merchandize which may have passed under the contract from the plaintiff to the defendant, without the least regard to the ruinous consequences that might follow, and without apparently taking the trouble to inquire into the question of what ground in any system of law they can have for such a demand.

In a word, then, in all applications to put goods of another party under sequestration, the person applying must make such a case on proved facts (that is, facts deposed and sworn to) as will satisfy the Court that he has a right to such an order, by the law of England. It is hard to be particular in directions on a subject which presents so many various cases, and in which the rule of action depends so much on the peculiar circumstances of each instance. Caution and

a disinclination generally to use extraordinary remedies, or extreme measures, are the best protection against serious mistakes.

Even more serious still is the responsibility which is cast occasionally (in some places very frequently) on the Consular authorities by applications to stop the clearances of ships. With regard to many of these, which are made by persons who have claims for work or supplies, they are, under the view taken here of the law, quite inadmissible. A shipwright has a lien on a ship *in his hands* for repairs; otherwise his remedy, like that of the ship-chandler for stores or supplies, is personal against the owner or captain who employed him.* It is, moreover a rule in the Supreme Court never to stop a ship under charter, while prosecuting a voyage. In all cases where the ship is in a port of destination there is, or ought to be, an agent who practically is generally prepared to give the necessary security to meet any claim. The only serious difficulty likely to arise is where the vessel is sought to be detained to answer large claims for compensation for injuries by collision, and the agent hesitates to pledge himself for so considerable an amount, or is not in a condition to satisfy so large a claim if found due. In such cases, on proper evidence establishing a *primâ facie* case, the claimant has a right to detain the ship until the claim can be heard and determined, or until proper security be given; but it is a legitimate condition to impose that the plaintiff should push on his claim with all dispatch, and do all in his power to have it tried on its merits within the shortest possible time.

<small>Stoppage of Ships.</small>

With regard to *ex parte* injunctions, all that it is necessary at present to say is, that they, also, are an extraordinary remedy, not to be in any case lightly granted; and in no case to be granted at all, unless a clear *primâ facie* case is made out, on facts properly deposed to, convincing the Court that by the law or practice of the Courts of Equity of England, or by the well-known and established local custom, the applicant is entitled to an order such as is applied for.

<small>Ex-parte Injunctions.</small>

I prefer putting the case in this way, to giving necessarily imperfect and unsatisfactory statements of the cases in which such applications would be granted at home, because a party asking for an extraordinary remedy ought to come fully prepared to show his right to it: and in the long run, less mischief will be done, by the frequent inability to obtain an injunction, than by anything which would approach to an indiscriminate granting of such orders.

It remains, on this branch of the subject, which I have treated at some length, but certainly at not more than its importance requires, to point out that even where, on one of the foregoing applications, such a case is made out, on written evidence, by affidavit (or affirmation where allowed by law), as convinces the Consul that an order ought to be made, it will be proper, in all those cases where the nature of the application permits it, only to make an "interim," or temporary order, to prevent at once the consequences which the applicant seeks to avert, but putting the applicant under terms to renew his application in the presence of the other party by motion

---

* But see 26 and 27 Vict. Ch. 24, Sec. 10—passed in 1863, and Page 14 ante. Title "Admiralty."

upon notice. Of course, this cannot apply to an application to hold to bail; and in this case, if an order is granted *ex parte*, it will be for the party affected by it to apply, as he may think fit, to have it rescinded.

In all cases a copy of the affidavit, or affidavits, and of the Consular order, must be served on the party against whom the application is made, and on the captain of any ship ordered to be detained.

When a claim or petition by which an order in any way affecting the interest of another party is presented, the speedy communication of it to that party becomes necessary.

Here it is an almost universal rule, that all service of orders, or copies of pleadings, takes place by the messenger of the Court, and for this service a fee is charged. This practice is necessary to prevent fraud; for where there is no professional class, as in England, who undertake on behalf of their clients to effect service of process, it is difficult, in the absence of the defendant, to proceed with the satisfactory conviction that he has had due notice; indeed, even in England, in the County Court practice, where, as a general rule, professional assistance is not pre-supposed, the same principle is acted on. The circumstances, however, under which the subjects of Christian Powers reside in this Empire, and the nature of the country, and difficulty of communication, make it impossible, even here always to adhere to this rule. Indeed, where the distance of the residence of the party is considerable, the staff at the disposal of the Court is quite inadequate to insure the service of process within a reasonable time. In these cases, therefore, the party interested is sometimes allowed to effect service himself, and must, then, when it is necessary, be prepared to satisfy the Court, on oath, of the time, place, and manner of the service. It is desirable to have this established with a degree of particularity which would make an unscrupulous person afraid to state a falsehood; but however positive the assertion of due service may be, if the Court is not satisfied, it will be better to take further measures for insuring the knowledge of the proceedings on the part of the defendant.

In order to act in any particular stage of a judicial proceeding in the absence of one of the parties whose right or duty it is to be present thereat, or in order to proceed in any suit in the absence and default of some step on the part of one of the litigants, which it would have been his right or duty to have taken on receiving due communication or notice of the order, pleading, or other process rendering the taking of such step his right or duty, the Court must be satisfied that there is a reasonable certainty that the proper notice came to the knowledge of the party at such a period as to give him a reasonable time for making his arrangements to be present or to take the particular step which he has not taken: or else, that he is wilfully keeping out of the way, or taking other measures, to avoid the service of the process of the Court. In the latter case, it would be the duty of the Court, before proceeding further, to direct that service should be effected on a particular person, or at some particular place, and that such service should be held good service on the party for the purposes of the suit. The circumstances of each particular case will almost invariably point out some course which will

prevent undue delay, and ensure knowledge on the part of the person to be served.

I have endeavoured to point out the principle on which the Court ought to act, and of course this principle is applicable to every stage of the proceedings where it is asked to proceed in default.

Let us suppose then that a defendant is properly served with a petition; if it is defective, he may (and ought, as we have seen) apply to the Court to have it either amended or set aside: if it is defective from want of particulars of demand, he ought to apply for them, and get them as of course; if it is confused and incomprehensible (a case here at least by no means uncommon), he ought to apply to the Court at once to force the plaintiff to put in a better and more intelligible petition, or to have his petition set aside; if it is full of irrelevant matter or abuse, he ought at once to apply on that ground to have it amended or set aside. The most convenient way of proceeding in these cases will probably be, that the party should obtain on application a summons or rule calling on the other side to show cause, on such a day, why the particular order asked for should not be made; and on the application for such a summons, which I think should be made within four days from the service of the petition, the Court ought to satisfy itself (in most cases a perusal of the petition will suffice), that there is some *primâ facie* ground for the application, and that the summons is not taken out merely for delay, or in a vexatious spirit. In England, the penalty of costs operates as a check on improper applications. Here the Court itself must, to a great extent, take care that the parties are not needlessly taken away from their avocations to answer frivolous objections.

<small>Proceedings after Service.</small>

Before altogether quitting this part of the subject, I ought to notice what may be said against the course I have suggested as the duty of the defendant, namely, that he should raise his objection at once to a defective petition. It may be said that this is, as it were, putting on the defendant, the task, in certain instances at least, of improving the plaintiff's case against himself, whereas, if he waited until the hearing a defective petition, especially if not answered at all, would in many cases result, at best, in a nonsuit. Again, it may be argued that in the English practice many of those petitions which I have included in the defective class would be so bad as to be fatal to the plaintiff's case at any stage of the proceedings, and indeed, generally, that the distinction between bad and defective petitions is unknown to the English procedure.

To all this I should answer that the object of all procedure in civil suits is to find out the several material questions of law and fact in dispute between the litigant parties, and put them "in issue;" and if there is a real question capable of being raised between the plaintiff and defendant, and which is material to be decided, it is a matter of mere expediency whether you will adopt the course of allowing that material question to be got at by necessary amendments where it has not at once been properly raised, or drive the plaintiff to another suit on the same subject matter. But in point of fact the principle of this method of procedure has been extensively adopted of late years in English practice, and I am convinced that here it is desirable to take all the means in the power of the Consular tribunals to encourage the parties to come to a clear understanding of what the questions between them really are, before the hearing.

I prefer the way I have suggested to the course adopted in many foreign systems, where, after a voluminous "plaidoyer" in writing, a preliminary hearing takes place to try and develope issues, the determination of which is referred to a future day. To this course there are many serious objections, besides those of expense and delay.

The Rules, however, enable the Court, on application of either party, to "settle issues," because in the absence of competent legal assistance it is sometimes difficult for the parties to perceive how narrow is the question in dispute. And the effect of this knowledge is to save trouble to the Court and expense to the litigants, and to prevent the necessity of their calling witnesses to prove facts really not disputed or wholly irrelevant; sometimes, even to stop the suit, by convincing one or other of the parties that on such an issue as the true issue has turned out to be, he can have no reasonable chance of success. I may remark that the settling of the issues between parties by an act of the Court, is a part of the procedure of the Scottish Courts.

A summons, however, to settle issues should ordinarily be granted only after an answer has been given to the petition or claim of the plaintiff; and before I say anything of what ought to be required in an answer, it will be necessary to consider that class of cases in which the defendant does not see fit to put in any answer at all.

The ordinary result of this course in the practice of the Supreme Court is, that it enables the plaintiff, after the time for answering has expired, to set down the cause in the hearing list; the defendant being supposed to deny generally the truth of every material allegation of fact in the petition, and also to deny the alleged legal consequence, namely, the right to the relief asked. The rules as to the limitation of the defence at the hearing, in cases where no answer has been put in, and those which prohibit defences inconsistent with the answer if put in, or otherwise likely to take the plaintiff by surprise at the hearing, are all founded on the same principle. The parties ought to know, with reasonable certainty, what the questions between them really are; the object of legal procedure ought to be to obtain for each one this knowledge from the other. The tricks of pleading and of "Nisi prius" trials are generally devoted to the purpose of hiding your own case until the last moment, so far as you can, and getting as much insight as possible into that of your adversary.

Suppose that a plaintiff sues the defendant for the price of certain goods sold and delivery to him; imagine that in reality the defendant has paid the sum demanded to a person on account of the plaintiff, whom he, the defendant, supposed to be authorized to receive it. Now, if he either does not answer at all, or simply answers that he "owes the plaintiff nothing" (a very common answer, but in no case allowed as a plea in England) he does nothing which advances the decision of the real point in dispute, namely, whether the payment so made was well made, or is nugatory as regards the plaintiff. By not answering at all, he puts the plaintiff to prove the delivery of the goods, and this he has an undoubted right to do, but

he does not give him notice of his substantial defence. By the other so-called answer, he particularizes nothing; for it may mean that he never got the goods, or that they were not the plaintiff's, or that he has paid for them, or that the plaintiff forgave him the debt, or in short, it may mean such a variety of things that it raises no issue.

If he had answered, "that he was never indebted to the plaintiff as alleged," that would, of course, raise certain distinct issues—as the property of the plaintiff, the delivery, and the price—but it would not at all raise this issue, namely, whether he had paid for them or not: and unless he had put that forward as a distinct and additional ground of defence, it is clear that he could not, without injustice to the plaintiff, be allowed at the hearing when the delivery and property were proved, to come forward and swear to a payment of which the plaintiff had never (I will assume) heard, to a person who may have left the plaintiff's service before that payment, and that with the knowledge of the defendant, or at all events under circumstances which made ignorance on the defendant's part inexcusable.

If a lawyer had answered for him, using the general terms ordinarily employed in pleading in Courts of Common Law in England, he might have put forward as his answer or plea, "that before the suit was brought, he paid the plaintiff," and this would be correct, if the person who had received the money had been really the plaintiff's authorized agent; but it would instantly have put the plaintiff, conscious that he had not been paid, to taking measures to discover the time, place, and method in which the alleged payment had been made. And if a non-professional man had answered straightforwardly, he would have probably advanced the issue still better than the lawyer, by saying, "in answer to Mr.———'s demand, I admit having received from him the goods he mentions, but beg leave to state that afterwards, on the   day of   I paid the sum now claimed as their price to his clerk Mr.———, and have his receipt." On receiving this answer, the plaintiff would come prepared (which otherwise he might not have been) at the hearing on the real question between the parties. By setting down the cause for hearing, he is taken, in the practice of the Consular Courts, to deny the fact of payment as alleged, and the authority of the person to whom it was made, to receive it, these being the material allegations in the answer; and he would, if the payment to the clerk was proved, and the character of the clerk as his agent made out *primâ facie*, be able, either by cross-examination, or substantive testimony, or both, to show that the character of agent had ceased before the defendant handed over the money, and that the defendant must be taken to have known that it had ceased, so far as would suffice to make him bear the loss of the money which had been paid indeed, but to a wrong person, and never received by the person entitled to it.

If a defendant does not answer at all, he cannot at the hearing complain that he is debarred from setting up any defence which depends on more than denial or argument, and which is founded on substantive facts which he must prove affirmatively, and might and ought to have set up beforehand; but the principle of preventing surprise is the safe guide in such matters, and the task must necessarily be thrown on those who have judicial functions to perform, of determining in what cases, where no answer has been put in, the interests of truth and justice require that the defendant should be allowed at a later stage to set up a defence he ought at once to have put forward. It should always be a condition of this indulgence that he should pay to the plaintiff the substantial reasonable costs to which the latter has been put, in consequence of a necessary adjournment; and in almost every case the plaintiff would have a right to ask for an adjournment, and proper notice of the new defence.

Many of these remarks will, of course, necessarily apply where the defendant, having put in some answer, attempts at the hearing to raise a defence inconsistent with it, or of a description which is not stated in it, and ought to have been specially set forth. The interests of truth must determine here what amount of indulgence should be granted, care being taken to prevent the plaintiff from having his position materially prejudiced by the consequent delay.

In England no such indulgence must be expected as of course, although the Judges hold and exercise most extensive powers of amendment and adjournment to secure justice; but the circumstances of the place make a broad distinction, and a gradual introduction of a stricter procedure, with a constant application of the principles on which the Rules are founded, will be the surest method of advancing the interests of truth. It is undesirable and unjust suddenly to enforce on a community peculiarly ignorant of law, the letter of a technical system, however well-founded or convenient in itself; but as the public becomes familiar with the principles and provisions of the Rules, a general and consistent adherence to them will be found to be the best course for all; uncertainty and caprice being almost the greatest evils possible in the administration of justice. Great latitude of discretion is necessary, and the Rules have been framed with a view to that necessity: but it should be the constant study of every judicial officer to avoid real inconsistency in the practice of his Court.

Proceedings on Answer.

The answer may be open to some of the same objections as the petition: it may be so confused, or uncertain, or irrelevant, as to afford the plaintiff no fair information as to whether some or all of the material facts stated by him are admitted or specifically denied, or passed over without notice, or confessed and avoided. The answer may be bad; that is, amounting to no answer. In one case in the Supreme Court, to a petition claiming a balance on an account stated between the parties, the defendant's answer was, "Instead of "making ridiculous demands upon me, Mr.———would do better "to remove his goods, which are lying at my house," &c., &c. And I think this style of answer used to be by no means uncommon. It is clear that this is really so far equivalent to no answer at all, that it admits nothing, denies nothing, and raises no substantive affirmative defence.

It is in such cases as these that it may be proper, on application, to get the parties before the Court and settle the issues between them.

Defences in "confession and avoidance" as they are technically termed, comprise those defences which admit the facts stated, but

set up some other matter by which the legal obligation therefrom resulting has been discharged, or, in certain cases, has never arisen, or may be avoided by reason of some other matter of law or fact not appearing on the face of the claim or petition. Payment is a defence in confession and avoidance; so is release; so is performance: co-verture and infancy are also specimens of the second kind of these defences.

In all these, and the other numerous instances of defences of this nature, there is this general feature, that some new material thing will have to be proved by the defendant at the hearing, by which the inference arising in the plaintiff's favour on the face of his petition will be defeated, or, technically, "avoided."

Thus, if a petition is filed, claiming payment of a debt from a person who has been discharged under the Bankrupt Act, or who is a married woman or who is under the age of twenty-one years, or of a debt which was contracted at a time, and under circumstances which, if stated, would give in law a right to the defendant to resist the payment; and these facts, or circumstances, are not respectively stated on the petition, the defendant must clearly state these facts or circumstances applicable to the particular case, and on which he intends to rely; and he must be ready to prove such facts at the hearing. And he ought to set up this defence by his answer, because it gives the plaintiff notice of the facts on which he intends to rely; and the plaintiff has a right to such notice to enable him to show that such facts do not constitute a defence by reason of some other circumstances which he may then be prepared to prove. Thus, if a defendant relies on the fact of his having been under twenty-one years of age at the time of the alleged debt having been contracted, the plaintiff may either desire to deny that fact, or to rely on the independent fact that the debt was incurred for "necessaries to the defendant;" or, if the defendant wishes to rely on the fact of the debt being barred by the statute of limitations (prescription), the plaintiff may desire to set up as against such defence a subsequent acknowledgment, or part payment, or some other fact which will destroy the effect of such defence. The object in all cases is to prevent any undue advantage by surprise.

Payment and release are simple instances. But suppose a claim on the promise of the defendant to pay money to the plaintiff in consideration of a certain thing. The defence is that a statute has made that particular thing illegal, or that it is illegal at common law. The defendant does not deny the promise, but sets up with his "confession" the matter of "avoidance," namely, the illegality of the consideration; and he ought to set it up if he intends to rely on it at the trial, as he ought to set up any other defence of which the burden of affirmative proof will lie on him. So if a man sued for money said to be due by him in respect of some mercantile transaction, intends to rely on misrepresentation or concealment or any kind of fraud by the plaintiff, common justice will suggest that he ought to plead them, or bring them forward in his answer, for he will have to prove them, and the other party is entitled to notice, to enable him, if he can, to rebut the proof.

With regard to placing distinct matters of defence before the

Court in the answer, this, of course, will often happen; because in truth, and in fact, there may be distinct and separate defences.

It will be observed in the Rules, that after answer no further pleading can take place. This is intended to prevent the endless interchange of documents which I have before referred to, and sounds much more arbitrary than it really is. In formal pleading, where competent professional men are engaged, the issue or issues will be most surely developed in a very short process; but inasmuch as the general use of a replication is to take issue on some particular material fact set up as a defence, and inasmuch as the absence of a replication in the practice of the Consular Courts would not operate as an admission of any fact in the answer, one great object of this particular pleading ceases. Moreover, as there is little hope between non-professional pleaders of the issue being strictly and formally brought out at the last, it seems convenient to stop the written communications at as early a stage as possible, and where there is a necessity for doing so, to get the parties before the Court before trial, to determine the point to try. And, when an answer sets up new facts to qualify or avoid the inference derived by the plaintiff from the allegations of the petition, the plaintiff will always have an opportunity of meeting the defence by amendment of the petition, where necessary.

Answer on Oath. In the English Chancery practice, where the defendant is bound to answer categorically, and on oath, the plaintiff's bill, the amendment of the bill after, and in consequence of the answer, is constant; indeed, one of the principal objects in our Equity system is, by searching the conscience of the defendant, to force him to declare the exact state of the case, so far as it lies within his knowledge or belief, and thus to help the plaintiff so to shape his case as to obtain relief, if equity (which does not mean abstract justice, but the doctrine of the Court) will entitle him to it on the true facts.

Amendments. Amendment ought to be liberally allowed, the reasonable charges to which the other party is put being borne by the party amending, and the Court being satisfied that they are applied for *bonâ fide*, and not for the mere purpose of vexation or delay.

Applications for further Time. No application for time beyond that allowed by the rules ought to be granted as of course. The judical officer must hold the scale even, and see that neither party is allowed to avail himself of a time rule to press his adversary unduly, or to obtain a relaxation of it for the purpose of delay.

I attach much importance to a conviction in the public mind, in places where there is much judicial business, that it is treated strictly in its turn, and that nothing except the consent of parties, or the absolute requirements of justice, will induce the Consul to allow a case to be hurried to a hearing, or not heard when its time comes.

Hearing. I think that the provisions of the Rules as to Hearing Lists should be observed as nearly as may be, in the great Consulates at least. All applications for postponement or advance of cases must be made either by consent or in the presence of the other side, and if not consented to, should be made to and granted by the person entrusted with judicial functions, and him alone.

And here I may naturally introduce the little I have to say on interlocutory applications generally. Interlocutory Applications.

It is a matter of indifference, perhaps, in many instances, whether these applications are reduced to writing before they are made to the Court, but I am decidedly of opinion that, if nowhere else, yet in the Consul's note-book of civil cases, the gist of every application which seeks to procure the issuing of some interlocutory order, should be recorded; and whether such application was or was not successful, the result ought to be noted. This will serve as a record for many purposes, not the least valuable of which will be to enable the Courts to preserve consistency of practice.

As a rule, obviously no order can be made affecting the interest of another party, without giving him an opportunity of being heard on the point; but there are many cases in which the Court, as I have elsewhere said, ought to take special means to protect parties from frivolous motions, by requiring *ex parte* applications for rules to show cause to be made in the first instance.

It does so happen occasionally that the whole object of a suit may be to obtain an order, which may be applied for on motion as soon as the suit is instituted; for instance, an order for an injunction. Useful, but dangerous, except in well skilled hands, is the power of granting orders of this nature, and yet it is in substance of a power that has been commonly exercised by Her Majesty's Consuls.

It is a delicate jurisdiction, and I see no reason for widening the rule I laid down in speaking of *ex parte* applications of this description : the person asking for such an order must show his title to it in the clearest way. But when a motion turns out to raise really the whole question in the suit, it would be proper for the Court to obtain, if possible, the consent of the parties to treat it as the hearing, so as to remove all necessity for suspending the judgment on any point, the parties being put to establish their final rights at once. In these cases it would always be proper to allow a short adjournment of the motion, on the demand of either party, for the purpose of procuring or completing evidence.

It is a matter of the utmost importance to impress on the minds of suitors, on every possible occasion, that their bounden duty is to attend at the hearing with all the written evidence and all the witnesses they may require in support of their respective cases; and that our procedure differs from the foreign systems where, after lengthy arguments, the presiding Judge determines what are the issues, and states judicially what evidence is to be produced on each point at a future day. They should be taught systematically that argument or statement, except on facts proved, or then and there about to be proved, can go for nothing at all, and that a man who, under the system of pleading to issue (which may be enforced substantially, however informally) comes with a knowledge of what he wants to prove, and what he may or will be required to disprove, is quite inexcusable unless he comes prepared at once with all his available testimony. Piecemeal trials are a great hardship. It is to be hoped that suitors in British Consular Courts may gradually be brought to have as little expectation of obtaining adjournment to produce testimony which they had every opportunity of bringing, Evidence to produced at Trial.

and should have known they ought to bring, at the trial, as they certainly would have in England; but I would lay down no inflexible rule in practice.

<small>Witnesses.</small>

It is one of the duties which society imposes on a man, that he shall be ready to give his attendance to assist justice by testifying to all facts within his knowledge: it is equally the duty of the Court, which obliges him to attend, to see that he has reasonable, even ample notice of the time when his attendance may be required.

Where foreigners are required as witnesses, it is necessary also to allow for the time consumed in communicating with them through their respective Consulates, which, so far as the experience of the Supreme Court can be trusted, enforce the attendance of their subjects at a foreign Court as witnesses with an enlightened readiness which does them honour. I have no doubt that British Consuls throughout China and Japan experience and afford the same facilities in these matters.

<small>Taking Depositions.</small>

A convenient and customary practice here, which I presume is in general use, allows the taking of the evidence of any particular witness (where the pleadings are concluded and the issues ascertained), in the presence of both parties, in any case where, from necessary approaching departure, or other reasonable cause, there is fair ground to suppose that the witness will be absent at the time of trial. The notes of the evidence are used at the trial, and as the witness has been subject to cross-examination, there is little, if anything, lost. The migratory character of the European subjects has rendered this practice necessary.

<small>Proceedings at the Hearing.</small>

At the hearing of a cause, the duty of the Consul, after having ascertained that both parties appear either in person, or by their representatives, is to decide, in case of dispute, which has the right to begin. This matter seldom has the importance here which is attached to it in England, and it is only for the sake of regularity in the proceedings, that it becomes worth while to give a few plain directions on the subject.

<small>Who to begin.</small>

The presiding officer has to consider what is the substantial fact to be made out, and on whom it lies to make it out. It is common to say, that the person who has the affirmative of the issue ought to begin; but the affirmative must be sometimes taken in a more extended sense than the word itself ordinarily implies. Thus, where a plaintiff sued for damages, arising from the unworkmanlike execution of a contract, and the defendant pleaded that the work was done in a proper and workmanlike manner, it has been held that the plaintiff should begin, as being the party who undertook to establish the substantial fact of the issue. And in an action claiming damages from the defendant, for not building certain houses according to specification, where he pleaded that he did build the houses according to the specification, it was held that the plaintiff should begin, and show that he did not.

In cases, such as I have before referred to, where there is a general denial on the part of the defendant of the plaintiff's cause of suit, and also a separate subtantive matter of defence, such as payment, set-off, release, and the like, the plaintiff must begin, because the first issue is to be made out by him, the defendant by his denial

having put him to the proof of it; and it is only on his making out that cause of suit, that the burden would lie on the defendant of establishing the substantive defence he has set up; but if the defendant has pleaded payment alone, or release alone, or the like, then of course, he ought to begin, and make out his plea, because he has confessed, and only seeks to "avoid" the plaintiff's claim, and he must show and prove how that is to be done.

When the proceedings are commenced, I cannot too strongly recommend all those whose duty it is to preside at them, to enforce regularity, to prevent interruption, and to make it constantly manifest to the parties and bystanders that the Court is proceeding by rule. *Regularity of proceeding must be enforced.*

It is thought here, that not only the English public, but even foreigners, are for the most part extremely sensible of the great facilities for arriving at the truth, which are secured by our English procedure in Court, which in principle would seem to be at once simple and natural.

The first special characteristic of the system is, that no statement of fact is of the least value unless it is either proved or admitted. In practice in England, where addresses are in almost every case made by Counsel, it is a strict rule that Counsel should not state any fact which he is not instructed to call evidence to prove; and the certainty of being called to account by his opponent and by the Judge, generally brings the deviations from this rule within tolerably narrow limits. In China and Japan, opening statements, especially by non-professional persons, are of little importance; but what is of great importance is, that the Court should act on proof or admission, and on nothing less. *Statement insufficient, Proof necessary.*

The method in which the proof is tendered is, I may fairly say, the best that exists. By the English law, with but a few exceptions, every person who has a direct personal knowledge of any material fact, can be called to testify, on his oath, to that fact. The restrictions which hamper evidence, and impede the discovery of truth, and which foreign codes seem destined to perpetuate in their respective countries, have, for all practical purposes, been swept away in English procedure: and no objection can be made to the competency (or admissibility) of a witness by reason of his being a party, or interested, or convicted of crime, or for any cause, except absolute incapacity of mind, or that which the law looks on as withdrawing all real security for truth—a disbelief, namely, in a state of retribution. Other objections do not go to the admissibility of the witness, but to the amount of credit which the tribunal will afford to his testimony. *Mode of tendering Proof.*

As a general rule, the testimony given ought to be *vivâ voce*, in the presence of the opposite party, and of the Court which has to decide the case; the witness' manner of telling his story is an integral—often an important—part of his evidence, and affords indications both of his impartiality and accuracy. Where necessity requires the use of the written deposition of a witness not taken by the Judge who has to decide the case, something is always lost:

Again, the evidence must be direct and positive; hearsay evidence (with exceptions not material to be noticed, as in matters of family *Hearsay Evidence.*

pedigree) is no evidence. If a witness were to commence an account by saying, "Mr. A. told me that the defendant said to him;" the obvious remark is, "Why have we not Mr. A. himself here to tell us what the defendant told him? If the defendant told you, the witness, anything, state that." If I may judge by personal experience here, however, the most usual manner in which this secondhand evidence is given or offered, is by a downright statement—"The defendant said"—and it is generally only in answer to a question by the Court, on the defendant's denial, that the witness admits that he is only speaking on another man's information. Now if the defendant really does deny the statement, it is the plainest justice that his denial should be good as against any person but one in whose presence the statement was made: and if the statement is material, it is the business of the plaintiff to secure the attendance of the very person to whom it was made, or to ask the defendant, if called as a witness, or, even—as an extreme measure—to call him himself for that purpose, if he ventures to trust either his conscience or his fear of consequences.

Statements by either party, to a third person, are not evidence for, although they are against, the party making them; but entries in a man's books of business, if proved to be regularly made in the ordinary course of business, are, by custom here, *primâ facie* evidence of the facts they purport to record.

All conversations between the parties having reference to any of the matters in issue, are evidence adducible by either.

The rules, indeed, of evidence, according to the English practice, are, although occasionally technical, founded on principles of common sense, being intended to secure the production of the *best* evidence of any fact, and not requiring stricter proof than ought, as a general rule, to be obtainable by a person whose deep interest makes him take pains to procure it.

I have no more intention, in this letter, of framing an unsatisfactory treatise on the law of evidence, than on any other branch of the law. I have merely pointed out the general elementary principles on which evidence ought to be received or rejected; and I am perfectly conscious that an unprofessional man endeavouring to administer strict technical rules, would be likely to do far more mischief than if he trusted to his natural common sense. The following propositions may, however, be offered as aids with respect to the admission or rejection of evidence.

Evidence.

Matters collateral and irrelevant to the questions raised on the pleadings should not be permitted to be given in evidence, but in cross-examination witnesses may be questioned on matters not in themselves relevant to the issue for the purpose of testing their credit.

No evidence should be permitted to be given in contradiction of a statement by a witness on a matter not material to the question or questions in issue between the parties, except the proof of a conviction of such witness for a criminal offence, in case he shall on cross-examination deny such conviction or refuse to answer.

Comparison of a disputed writing with any writing proved to the satisfaction of the Court to be genuine is permitted to be made by

witnesses, and such writings and the evidence of witnesses respecting the same may be submitted to the Court as evidence for or against the genuineness of the writing in dispute.

The burthen of proof lies on the party who substantially asserts the affirmative of the issue between the parties. On whom burthen of proof lies.

The party who must fail on the allegations contained in the pleadings if no evidence were given on either side, or the party who must fail if any one or more allegation or allegations contained in the pleadings, respecting which it is doubtful who should prove the same were struck out, may be taken as that party on whom the proof lies.

The evidence required for the proof of any fact requiring to be established, should be the best of which the case in its nature is susceptible.

Primary evidence is that which on the face of it carries no indication that better remains behind.

Secondary evidence is that which itself indicates the existence of more original sources of information.

No evidence ought to be received which is secondary or substitutionary in its nature so long as the original evidence is attainable.

The contents of a written instrument which is capable of being produced should be proved by the instrument itself and not by "parol" evidence.

If any written instrument be destroyed or lost, the party seeking to give secondary evidence of its contents, must give some evidence that the original once existed, and must either prove its destruction positively, or by a reasonable presumption, as by showing that it has been thrown aside as useless or the like, or he must establish its loss by proof of search made without effect, but with reasonable diligence in the place or places where it was most likely to be found. Secondary Evidence.

Such search need not necessarily be recent or for the purposes of the case.

The contents of documents deposited in foreign countries or elsewhere out of the jurisdiction of the Court, and of any records of judicial Courts and entries in public books or registers, including the books of notaries public, may be proved by legalised or otherwise certified copies thereof. Legalized Copies.

The contents of any document in the possession or power of the adversary who withholds it at the hearing may be proved by secondary evidence, provided that a proper notice (when requisite) to produce the original has been given to such adversary.

Notice to produce should to contain sufficient information to induce the party reasonably to believe that a particular writing will be called for, either by itself or as forming part of a class or collection mentioned in the notice, and in such case is sufficient without particularizing every writing.

If any original writing is in Court, although the party proposing to prove its contents has not given notice to produce it, it may be called for, and if not produced, secondary evidence of its contents may be given.

If the nature of the suit, or the form of the pleadings, is such that the defendant must know he will be charged with the possession of some instrument, and be called on to produce it, secondary evidence may be given of the contents of such instrument, although no notice to produce has been given.

Secondary evidence of the contents of any writing may be given without notice to the adversary to produce the same, if it is proved to the satisfaction of the Court, that such writing has been forcibly or fraudulently obtained or taken possession of by the adversary, or obtained by him with a view to prevent its being given in evidence.

Any merchant seaman may bring forward evidence, to prove the contents of his agreement with the master of the ship or otherwise to support his case, without producing or giving notice to produce the agreement itself or any copy of it.

Notice to produce is not necessary where the adverse party, or his duly appointed attorney or his counsel, has admitted the loss of the document, but secondary evidence of the contents of such document may be given at once.

Secondary evidence of the contents of any writing is admissible, when it has been established to the satisfaction of the Court, that such writing is in the possession of a person whom the Court cannot compel to produce it, and who has been either summoned, or formally requested, to produce the same, and refuses to do so; and secondary evidence is admissible in such cases, whether the person who has possession of the writing is justified in not producing the same, or is not so justified, but only protected by want of jurisdiction in the Court.

Evidence given by a witness must be confined to facts within the knowledge of such witness of things said or done, and may not be extended to matters of which he has derived his information from others.

Evidence of declarations or statements, oral or in writing, made by any party to a suit, cannot be received in favour of such party.

Evidence of declarations or statements, oral or in writing, by any person not a party to the suit, cannot be taken as showing the truth of such declarations or statements, otherwise than where they are receivable by the law of England, as in matters of general reputation, matters of public interest, or family pedigree, and in cases of declarations against interest, and declarations in the course of business, as herein-after stated.

Evidence of a statement oral or in writing, made by a person since deceased against his own pecuniary or proprietary interests, may be received in suits between other parties, subject to the consideration of its greater or less value from the presence or absence of any competent or particular knowledge of the particular facts stated by the person making the declaration.

Such declaration may be received in evidence of collateral and independent matters forming part of the declaration, although not in themselves against the interest of the declarant.

Statements and declarations whether oral or in writing by persons not parties to the suit, if made in the ordinary course of the business of the individual making the same may be given in evidence.

Cross-examination, as used in our Courts, is altogether a distinctive feature of the English procedure. Where cases are conducted,

as often occurs here, by English counsel, its value and power are very greatly appreciated by foreigners, who admit its force as an engine for sifting testimony. In the absence of competent persons, however, it is a duty which the interests of truth cast sometimes on the Court, which, however, is bound to be careful to guard against the antagonistic spirit likely to arise in the breast of every cross-examiner. The questions asked by the Court of witnesses ought to be confined to those which a competent legal man would be sure to ask in cross-examination, on the evidence given.

When a witness is taken in hand by the Court, which should not be done until the parties have finished with him, the Judge ought not, for the sake of regularity, to allow any re-examination on the answers given to the Court; but it is proper to put any material question suggested by either party, if it tends to clear up a fact left in doubt.

It is the Judge's duty to take such a note of the evidence given, as will afford a record of the facts on which the Judgment is based. I am far from meaning that a Consul is bound, in every case he tries, to take down verbatim what every witness says; but the very fact of taking a note of the evidence as it is given, tends to promote regularity, and in cases brought up by appeal, a copy of the Judge's notes enables the Court above to see whether the judgment can be supported, and if not, whether the proper course is to give judgment for the other side, or to send the case to a new trial. These notes ought, in every case of appeal, to accompany the "record," that is, the pleadings and the judgment. It would be hard to say what an amount of difficulty to the Court, and hardship and delay to parties, has taken place, principally in appeals, from the systematic absence of any notes of evidence. Where any tangible objection is made to the reception of evidence, it ought to appear on the notes. And it should also appear whether the objection was allowed, overruled, or withdrawn by the party making it. This will assist the Court above in case of appeal. It is right, however, that the public and the Consuls should be aware that the Supreme Court will not disturb judgments on appeal for mere irregularity, if satisfied that substantial justice has been done between the parties. To act otherwise, would be to inflict great hardship on suitors, and would, in the public eye, cast an undeserved slur on gentlemen who do not pretend to administer justice either with the advantages of a professional education, or under circumstances where forms can be always followed. It remains only to say, on the subject of notes of evidence, that as the Supreme Court will accept them as conclusive, a strict obligation is cast on the Consuls to see that they are really what they profess to be—the pith and substance of the evidence given. In heavy and important cases, it would be desirable to take a pretty full note.

Importance of Judge's Notes of Evidence.

There is a natural tendency in parties (and it sometimes extends to their professional advocates) to go off into collateral issues, which do not bear on or assist the inquiry in which the Court is really engaged; the Judge should repress this; but where there is any doubt whether the evidence is not material to the true issue, it will be safer to admit it. It is admissible, for instance, to call a witness to contradict the evidence of another on a point material to the issue, but not on a collateral fact. Thus, if in cross-examination you ask a man, who has given account of a particular admission by the plaintiff of payment, whether he did not tell one A. B. that the plaintiff never admitted any such thing to him, and he denies that he told A. B. so, you call A. B. to swear that he did, for this is highly material to the issue; but if you, in cross-examination, had asked whether the same witness had not been discharged from the service of the plaintiff's brother on an accusation of dishonesty, and he denied it, you could not call the plaintiff's brother to prove the fact, for otherwise you might embark in, and have to try a hundred collateral issues, more or less irrelevant.

Judgments. With regard to judgments, the present form given in Consular Courts seems rather cumbrous, and is probably intended, by a "résumé" officially made, to supply the want of notes of evidence. If these exist, as they ought to exist, there seems no reason why Consular judgments should be the lengthy documents they are. Append to the record of the pleadings a simple statement of the hearing—the presence of the parties, or the service on the defendant if the cause was heard in his absence, and the conclusion or judgment of the Court.

The evidence is no part of the record, except for purposes of appeal—neither are the reasons for the judgment, if reduced to writing. It is often, in important cases, a very salutary practice for a Judge to write his reasons for his judgment; it forces him to put his mental conclusions more deliberately before himself, and to see more clearly how far they will fairly carry him.

In all cases of appeal, where written reasons for the judgment by the Consul himself accompany the notes of evidence, they will meet from the Supreme Court the utmost attention.

The formal judgment should, as I have said, be appended to the pleadings, so that the record may be complete; and it should be headed like all other papers in the suit, with the name of the Court, and the several names of the respective plaintiffs and defendants. The loose practice of putting as plaintiffs or defendants the names of firms, such as A. B. *and Co.*, has given rise to serious difficulties in execution. Wherever anything of this kind is discovered, it should be amended by the insertion of the real names of the several parties; if they are very numerous, it will be sufficient to insert them all in the petition, and head the *subsequent* papers:

{ Between A. B. and others, plaintiffs;
{ C. D. and others, defendants;

but the Court should always be able to ascertain, with certainty, who are defendants and who plaintiffs. The powers of amendment in these and other particulars given by law to persons presiding at the trial of civil cases, are very extensive, and they should be used freely to ensure the trial of every question on its real merits; that is the great object: subject to this, the Court ought to take care to avoid prejudicing the position of the opposite party by any amendment; and where it raises anything substantially new, he would be generally entitled to adjournment and real costs.

Contempt of Court. It is to be observed that Consular Courts are Courts of Record,

and have the power of preserving order, and the respect due to them, by commitment and fine. The very existence of such a power presupposes temper, patience, and discretion, in the person entrusted with it. And it is worthy of remark that, where the power is most extensive and undoubted, as in the Supreme Courts at Westminster, there is the least occasion for its exercise. Since the establishment of the Supreme Court, there has been only one commitment for contempt, and that contempt was manifest prevarication in a witness at a criminal trial. And notwithstanding this, the summons of the Court, even on criminal charges, is obeyed with such certainty, that it is very seldom either necessary or proper to bring a man up on a warrant. The experience of this city would seem to establish the fact that British subjects are peculiarly amenable to any mild but firm authority. But how much of this is owing to a consciousness of protection against the local authorities, and that such protection may depend on obedience to Consular rule, is another question.

The decree of the Court at the hearing is either final or interlocutory.

A final decree should ordinarily be made where the claim is for debt, or damages, whether for breach of contract or for a wrong independent of contract, and where there is no answer, or where the answer is in bar of the demand. Decree.

Interlocutory decrees at the hearing may be made in those cases in which, from the nature of the suit or of the decree which the Court, on the hearing, may consider itself bound to make, something remains to be done before the rights of the parties in relation to the question raised in the suit can be fully ascertained and declared. Interlocutory Decree.

An interlocutory decree should set forth the several matters necessary to be ascertained, and should provide for the manner in which they are to be ascertained.

It should also, wherever the same is possible, fix a time within which such matters are to be ascertained, and should give liberty to the parties respectively to apply to the Court, either to enlarge such time, or for any other purpose, as they may see occasion.

The execution of judgments for debt or damages presents peculiar difficulties here. If an appeal is possible, the unsuccessful party, for the most part, gives notice of appeal; for, not being afraid of any substantial costs, he avails himself of appeal as possible means of delay, or of driving his adversary to a compromise. If an appeal is not allowed by law, or if provisional execution of the judgment is ordered pending the appeal, the common course appears to have been for the debtor to declare himself in a state of insolvency, and seek an adjudication of bankruptcy, or the benefit of protection, with the simple purpose of obtaining personal protection, and of defeating the particular judgment creditor, but without the least expectation of complying with the provisions of the law in other respects. Execution of Judgments.

That protection from arrest has, in these cases been granted almost uniformly, is, I believe, undoubted; and when it is considered that, in most instances, a Chinese or Japanese prison is the only alternative, I at least can scarcely censure this practical abolition of imprisonment for debt, even though, in fact, after protection, if there was no estate, all proceedings mostly ceased; but considering that the difficulty of following property amongst so many different jurisdictions is so great as generally to make execution against goods practically ineffective, the Supreme Court has not hesitated to make two or three salient examples by allowing the law of arrest to take its course in these cases, and not granting protection until the debtor had practically learnt that he could not with impunity set the judgment of the Court at defiance.

Imprisonment. The rules establish an important modification of the system of imprisonment under decrees in civil suits. There will no longer be a power in the creditor at his own option to imprison his debtor under the decree, by way of execution of the decree. There will be no imprisonment except under a special order of the Court. Imprisonment so ordered will be for not more than 40 days at a time, and will be not in the nature of execution, but in the nature of imprisonment for an offence, as it will be inflicted only in the cases of proved fraud or misconduct on the part of the debtor. One consequence of the change is, that imprisonment will no longer operate as a satisfaction and extinguishment of the debt or liability, in respect of which the debtor is imprisoned.

The rules on this subject are substantially in conformity with the practice which has for some time existed in England respecting small debts, and which has been adopted in the County Courts there.

Execution on Goods. If there is property belonging to the debtor within the jurisdiction, the creditor has an absolute right to have it seized and sold in satisfaction of the decree; but the greatest care must be taken to avoid responsibility on the part of the Consulate in taking goods in execution, which should never be done except at the *express risk*, and by the direction of the execution creditor, and even then only when the Consul is satisfied as to the ownership of the property, or that the creditor is well able to meet the claim for damages in case of possible mistake. Where there is any doubt of the nationality of the property, the Consulate should on no account run the risk of embroiling itself with foreign Consulates, which here, at least, have been found perfectly ready to co-operate for the purpose of defeating fraudulent collusions. No personal responsibility of the judgment creditor would be an excuse to them for the seizure of the property of their subject: but on these occasions the Consulate may fairly insist that property, apparently and obviously in the order and disposition of the debtor, shall be secured until the foreign claimant has, within a short reasonable time, established his claim.

There are certain occasions in which the execution of the order of the Court may be enforced by the officers of the Consulate directly, as in giving possession of a British ship, or delivering a British subject from the illegal custody of another, or a foreigner from the illegal custody of a British subject. This has sometimes to be done in cases where young girls have been enticed into and are detained in houses of ill-fame. And the order to bring them up, if disobeyed, should be executed *by force* in cases where the house is British.

In many instances, from the peculiar relation of European inhabitants to the country in which they reside, the Court has no rightful jurisdiction over the thing in dispute, or from which satisfaction

for a judgment is sought, and must enforce its decree, if at all, by compelling the person over whom it has jurisdiction, and who is really able to deal with the thing, either to deal with it as he is bound to do by virtue of some obligation which the Court has a right to enforce; or, as the case may be, in other instances, to bring the value of the thing within the Court's jurisdiction, by selling under the Court's direction, and bringing in the proceeds.

In some cases there is no way of enforcing the orders, except by committing the party not obeying them; and the jurisdiction is so delicate, that I should strongly recommend a reference to the Supreme Court, with a copy of the pleadings and evidence in the case, before making any such decree.

There is no probability that the ordinary Consular Courts will be troubled with applications for new trials in cases heard before them. The losing party, if not intending to submit to the judgment, would probably use his right of appeal to the Supreme Court. *New Trials.*

The petitions and other papers filed by the parties for the purposes of appeal, will often, no doubt, contain a variety of assertions as to alleged facts which not only do not appear on the notes of evidence, but do not exist except in the imagination of the party. As an appeal will in most cases be decided on the evidence already given in the Court below, and as that evidence is proved by the notes of the Consul, I have already pointed out the obligation to be accurate. If, however, some fact is stated which was sworn to at the trial, but by accident the evidence was not noted, the Consul would, in transmitting the record of appeal, certify that he remembers that such fact was proved, with any observation that may occur to him on the point. The parties are to understand that the petition, or (in case of appeal by motion) the argument (if any) filed, will be treated as arguments on existing facts which appear to have been proved or admitted at the trial, or on matters of fact which took place at the trial, appearing on the notes of the Consul, and that the Court above will consider them, and decide on the whole case; also, that it is not necessary either to appear themselves before the Court or to instruct Counsel to answer their case there, *unless* they desire it. Appeals will be entered as they are received, and considered in turn, if the fees have been duly paid, and the judgment of the Court thereon will be transmitted to the Consul for the information of the parties. *Appeals.*

When a party proposes to appeal from an interlocutory order of a Consular Court, it is altogether in the discretion of the Consul whether he will at all delay the prosecution of the suit, to wait for the decision of the Supreme Court; but in transmitting such an appeal, he should inform the Court whether further proceedings have been stayed or otherwise.

In those cases, on appeal from a final decree, where the Court may deem it advisable to admit fresh evidence, it will usually send down an order to the Consul to take the evidence and to transmit the notes of it; and his duty will be to examine the witnesses, after notice to both parties to attend, in the same manner as if the examination were at the original hearing.

Provision is made in the Rules (*See Rule* 64) for preventing one party from keeping a suit, as it were, hanging over the head of *Compelling Proceedings in Cases Commenced.*

another for an indefinite period, without proceeding to have it heard and decided.

In exercising the power conferred on the Consular Courts in this particular, it is necessary to remember that there may be causes not discovered by the plaintiff until after he has instituted his suit, which render him naturally and not unfairly desirous of postponing the hearing. Thus, for instance, the loss of a material document which he thinks he can recover, or the departure of a material witness whose return is not certain, but whose presence at the trial would be much more desirable than his written deposition; or again, the desire to avoid the expense of a Commission to examine witnesses; all these induce him to avoid going to trial as long as possible.

It will be for the Court to decide whether or not the delay is reasonable; and it is only when the delay is clearly harassing or prejudicial to the defendant that the trial should be peremptorily forced on.

Power to bar future proceedings. A very stringent power is sometimes exercised by the Supreme Court of making an order in certain cases barring further proceedings in the same cause of suit; local circumstances here, and the absence of any substantial scale of costs, as between party and party, have led to a practice by litigious persons of bringing suit after suit on the same cause, and either abstaining from proceeding to trial on any, or else so withdrawing from the suit before the conclusion as to avoid a judgment for the defendant, which would operate as a bar to a future demand. As a general rule it is and ought to be the right of the plaintiff to elect to be nonsuited at any time before the conclusion of the case by the Judge's verdict; but experience has shown here that a power ought to be left in the hands of the Court to bring litigation on one subject matter to a close, where it is evidently pursued for the sake of vexation. I cannot recommend, however, non-professional judges to attempt to make an order barring future proceedings, were the plaintiff desires to be non-suited, without a special application on the subject to the Supreme Court; and, indeed, there is every reason to hope that a fair scale of costs will so far operate as a check as to make this provision practically needless after some time.

How to get rid of long pending proceedings. Somewhat similar remarks will apply to the power of bringing existing suits to a close. In every Court there are some "opprobria" of justice of this kind—things which have remained either altogether, or for all'useful purposes, stationary for lengthened periods, and which are likely so to remain without the active interference of the Court. Some instances occur here where the application of different systems of law to different parts of the same case, the apathy of some parties, and the chicane of others, have produced a confusion not easily remediable.

It will be right for Consuls to whose attention the state of a suit of long standing may be brought, where no one appears inclined either to advance or to abandon it, to apply to the Supreme Court for direction, where they do not see their way clearly to make the parties get it decided. It will be the duty of the Court, however ungrateful and disagreeable the task, to examine the state of the cause, and direct the Consular Court how to act.

It will frequently happen that the same subject-matter will give rise to a suit and cross-suit. Sometimes it will be proper to take measures for hearing both on the same day; sometimes it will be sufficient not to issue execution in one suit until the event of the cross-suit is known. The circumstances of each case must guide the discretion of the Court. (*See Rule* 55.) Cross Suits.

Where there is no separate Equity jurisdiction, it must frequently have happened that an "equitable" defence would be set up to a legal claim, and that may be done in the answer, or by a cross-petition. In the former case, if the "equity" is established, it would sometimes be proper to give the consequent relief to the defendant on the hearing of the cause, but in other instances he might fairly be required to file a cross-petition. Equity.

There is considerable difficulty in even speaking of equitable defences to claims, without being greatly misunderstood by persons who have been rather accustomed to look on Equity as implying that natural justice which ought to be the foundation of all law, than as a collection of principles reduced to a strict and often technical system, and when a person considers he has to administer natural justice, he is too apt to make his own caprice the measure of it. Yet an "equitable" jurisdiction, in the professional sense of the word, has always been, and must always be, exercised by the Consular tribunals, for when the importance and complication of the questions which frequently are submitted to these Courts are taken into consideration, and also in some instances the magnitude of the interests involved, all that large and beneficial system which is known in England under the name of Equity cannot be ignored. And it is expressly provided by the Order in Council that a Consular Court shall be a Court of Law and of Equity.

The tendency of recent legislation has been to invest Courts of Law with many "equitable" powers, but there is no fusion of the systems in England. An example of a recent case of an "equitable" defence to an action at law will afford an illustration of the distinction between the systems, and I do not know any reason why such a case might not have come in substance under the judicial action of any of the Consulates here. Equitable Defences.

A bequest of money was made to a married woman, to her sole and separate use, independent of the control of her husband, her sole receipt being the discharge to the executor of the will. Instance of

This is one of those bequests which a Court of Equity will see carried into execution according to the intention of the testator, and the Court will restrain the husband from intermeddling with it, although in a Court of Law money comming to a married woman would instantly be considered as belonging to her husband.

In this case the wife directed the executor to pay the money to one C, she giving, on such payment, her separate receipt, and she disposed of it by appointing it to be held on certain trusts, under which her husband took no interest whatever.

The husband afterwards brought an action in a Court of Law against C, for money had and received to the use of him the husband, and the defendant certainly was without any answer at Law, because the money had and received by him to the use of the wife, was, in point of law, the property of the husband, and he would have to show the husband's authority for disposing of it.

Before the Common Law Procedure Act, 1854, the defendant C would have been forced to file a bill in Chancery, setting out the facts, and praying for an injunction to restrain the husband from proceeding with his action at law: but under that Act, which allows the pleading of "equitable" defences in an action at law, he pleaded the facts, nearly as I have stated them, as an equitable defence, setting out that he never received any money to the use of the plaintiff, except as aforesaid, thus identifying the transaction in respect of which he was sued with that in which he had received the money by direction of the plaintiff's wife; and the plea was held by the Court of Queen's Bench to be a good plea.

But observe, that it was a good "equitable" defence only because it was a defence that a Court of Equity would recognize as a ground for interfering with the proceeding at Law, and which it would force the plaintiff at Law to respect, however the action went.

Thus, in a case where an action was brought to recover money for freight and porterage, for the conveyance of goods, and for work done and materials provided, the defendant pleaded as an equitable defence that the plaintiff's claim was for work done by him as a bargeman employed by the defendant, and that in the course of that employment plaintiff undertook to carry certain coal of the defendant, and by negligence lost it; that the value of the coal was equal to the amount of plaintiff's claim, and defendant claimed "equitably" to set off the value of the coal lost against the plaintiff's claim. This plea was demurred to as bad: and the Court held that it was no good equitable defence, but a subject for a cross-action, on the ground that there was no recognized doctrine of Equity which would induce the Court of Chancery to interfere and restrain the plaintiff from prosecuting his action. Under the circumstances, an injunction would have been refused, if asked for, and the defendant would have been left to bring an action for damages for the loss of the coal. There appears to be an absence of natural connection between the two demands, which would render it proper to leave the defendant to establish the employment and negligence of the plaintiff, the loss of the coals and their value, in a separate demand. And although it might be proper to suspend execution in one action until the other was tried, and, if necessary, to set off one judgment against another, it would be introducing confusion to try two such distinct claims in the one action.

It might, however, be proper in a case where a defence to an action on a bond or bill clearly establishes the right of the defendant not only to succeed in the particular action, but to have the instrument delivered up to be cancelled, to make an order for that purpose without putting the defendant to file a petition to ask for such an order, even though in his answer he may not have suggested his title to that specific relief.

Specific Performance. The power of compelling what is called "specific performance" of contracts, is one which, probably, Consular Courts will be seldom asked to exercise. And the cases likely to occur in which such relief ought to be granted will be few indeed.

I should say of these applications, as I said of injunctions, that the safer course will be never to grant them, unless a strict technical right to them is established; at least, without a reference to the Supreme Court. A remedy in damages for non-performance is in general sufficient.

This observation, however, does not include a certain class of cases where orders may properly be made for the specific delivery up of certain goods known to be in the defendant's possession or control, and proved to be improperly detained by him from the plaintiff.

Cases do arise where such an order is equally just and expedient, and where it ought to be made, although Courts of Law in England would only give damages estimated according to the value of the goods.

It appears to be absolutely necessary to give a power to Consular tribunals to award costs of a substantial nature, but according to a recognized scale, as between party and party. It is fair that a party should be indemnified by his adversary for the reasonable expenses of enforcing a just or resisting an unfounded claim. It is expedient that a check should be put upon vexatious litigation by the knowledge that the expenses on both sides will have to be borne by its promoter. Costs should not be a matter of course; but there is no power the due exercise of which requires more freedom from caprice than that of awarding or refusing them. *Costs.*

In all judgments, whether interlocutory or final, some direction should be given about costs, even although in the former instances the direction will frequently only be, that the costs are to be costs in the cause. And in the Consular Courts generally, it will be proper that the amount allowed should be taxed, or ascertained and certified by the Consul himself. They are recoverable as a judgment debt; and where the payment of costs is made a condition precedent to the liberty to do any particular act, this condition should be strictly observed.

The costs of professional assistance should not be allowed except where real professional assistance has been given, and then only when there appears to the Court to have been a reasonable necessity for it, either from the nature or from the importance of the question between the parties.

I know no better way of discouraging the voluminous pleadings which have afflicted the Court and public here than by refusing to allow their expense, not only between party and party, but between attorney and client, when the bill of the former is disputed, as often happens, by the latter.

It would be desirable if, in the great Consulates, something like a roll of recognized practitioners could be established; but I see little chance of the business at any of the Provincial Courts being of a nature to attract men of ability or standing—as soon as the new system is more firmly established and fulfils the object for which it was brought into existence, the Chief or Assistant Judge of the Supreme Court will probably make an annual Circuit to the Chief Consulates and then in all probability the Bar of that Court will follow him. *Practitioners.*

The duty of deciding civil cases without the intervention of a jury, *Damages.*

which is cast upon Consular tribunals, makes it more especially necessary that Consuls should endeavour to understand the principle on which damages should be given: they are, indeed, placed in a position of most exceptional responsibility in this respect. A Judge presiding at a trial in England is well qualified to instruct the jury as to the principle on which they ought to proceed in assessing damages; and, in fact, they have the benefit of his judgment, learning, and experience brought home to the particular case in hand. A County Court Judge in England has the functions of a jury cast on him in many cases; but he is a professional man of experience, and his jurisdiction altogether, except by consent, is extremely limited; in addition to which, it may be observed, that in almost every case of importance, where there is any question fit for a jury, it is the interest of one party or the other to apply for it, and the judge is, in fact, assisted by a jury. It has, it is true, been thought right to oblige the Judges of the Superior Courts in England to try cases without a jury on the consent of parties, but there appears to be an extreme disinclination on all sides to resort to this course.

All suits to recover money seek it either in debt or in damages, and the damages sought may be either a sum certain or a sum "unliquidated," that is, unascertained. In any action of debt, and in the former of the two classes of claims for damages, the plaintiff seeks to recover a specific sum; and the duty cast upon the Court *quoad* the amount for which judgment should be given, is simply to ascertain whether the plaintiff has proved the whole or only a part of the claim, or whether the defendant has rebutted the proof of any part thereof, or has shown any reason for diminishing the amount, whether by partial failure of consideration, payment, set-off, or other defence, as to part.

A question, however, will often arise in these cases as to whether interest, which may be regarded as a species of real damages or compensation for the detention of the debt, ought to be allowed to the plaintiff.

In most petitions, whether to recover a debt or to recover damages for breach of contract, and whether the damages be a sum certain or be really unliquidated, interest is pretty sure to be specially asked for; and it becomes important to go even into detail to inform Consuls of what the state of the English law on this subject is, and in what cases they are obliged, in what allowed, and in what not allowed to grant interest as part of their judgment.

By an important Act passed in the reign of King William the Fourth—being "An Act for the amendment of the Law," it is provided: "That upon all *debts* or *sums certain*, payable at a certain "time, or otherwise, the jury, upon the trial of any issue or on any "inquisition of damages, may, if they shall think fit, allow interest "to the creditor at a rate not exceeding the current rate of interest, "from the time when such debts or sums certain were payable, if "such debts or sums be payable by virtue of a written instrument "at a certain time; or, if payable otherwise, then from the time "when demand of payment shall have been made in writing, so as "such demand shall give notice to the debtor that the interest will

"be claimed from the date of such demand until the term of pay-
"ment; *provided that interest shall be payable in all cases in which it
"is now payable by law.*"

On which it may be observed—first, that it does not extend to any action on contract which is brought *strictly* for the recovery of *unliquidated damages*. Secondly, that it is discretionary in the jury (or Judge exercising the functions of a jury) to allow interest even in the cases specified. Thirdly, that there is no discretionary power to award interest unless there be proof of a written instrument, whereby the debt or sum certain is made payable at a certain time, or proof of a written demand of the money, containing a notice that interest will henceforth be claimed. And fourthly, that interest *must* be given in all those cases in which it was payable by law at time when this Act was passed.

<small>No interest on unliquidated damages.</small>

The general common law rule is, that the law does not *imply* a contract on the part of a debtor to pay interest on the sum he owes, although the debt may be of fixed amount, and may have been frequently demanded. Nor is interest due as a matter of right in the absence of an express stipulation, even in the case of written instruments, unless they be commercial instruments of a negotiable nature, such as bills of exchange and promissory notes. It is not of *right* on a claim for goods sold, although the price was to have been paid on a certain day, or on a balance struck on an account for *goods sold* (although it *is* of right on an account stated between parties for *money lent*), or on a debt due for work and materials, or for money lent to or paid for the defendant, or had and received by him for the plaintiff's use, not even although it had been fraudulently received. It is not *necessarily* payable on a guarantee, or on a sum insured on a ship or on life, or on an attorney's bill, or upon a deed or covenant for the payment of money, unless amounting to a bond, or upon a sum due on a balance of accounts, or in most cases on money deposited with a banker.

But at common law, in the case of bills of exchange and promissory notes, the claim to interest is supported by mercantile usage: the acceptor of the bill and the maker of the note are respectively liable to pay interest thereon in the nature of damages from the time the instrument became due, even although interest be not reserved on the face of it, and there be no proof of any demand of payment: and in case of a note payable on demand, the plaintiff is entitled to recover interest from the time of the commencement of his action.

<small>Interest on Bills of Exchange.</small>

A banker's cheque carries interest, and the drawer or indorser of a bill, or the indorser of a note, is liable to pay interest from the time he receives notice of the dishonour. It has been held, that if there be a contract to pay a debt by a bill of exchange or promissory note, and the debtor refuses to give it, the plaintiff may recover interest on the amount from the time when the instrument, if given, would have become due, as part of the debt or damages; and the reason of this decision is obvious, for he contracted for that which would have made him liable to pay interest from the time referred to. But if the delay in paying a bill or note has been occasioned by the default of the holder, or the claim has lain dormant for a long time without any demand by him, the Court may and (without a good excuse in the latter case as between the parties) ought to refuse to allow interest: and where the holder of a bill died intestate, and no administration was taken out at once, it was held that the acceptor of a bill was not chargeable with interest, except from the time when the administrator, as the only person legally entitled, demands payment of the principal.

On Awards. Money payable under an *award* carries interest from the day on which it was payable, if recovered in a civil action.

On Bonds. A bond conditioned for payment of money impliedly carries interest from the time of the default which enables it to be put in suit, but not to an amount making the whole sum recoverable exceed the penalty.

A surety compelled to pay a sum of money is entitled to recover interest thereon, if his obligation to pay arose from his principal's default.

Compound Interest. There is no title to *compound* interest, except from expressed contract, or a contract implied from the mode of dealing with former accounts, or custom. And it has been decided that a customer is not bound or affected by the practice of his bankers to charge interest upon interest, unless it be proved that he was aware that such was their custom. It has been held by the House of Lords, that in *England*, a contract or promise for compound interest is not available, except, perhaps, in the case of mercantile accounts current for mutual transactions.

As a general rule, interest is allowed if there be a contract for the payment thereof, and an agreement between the parties that it should be paid may be inferred from the course of dealing, as, if it has been frequently charged and paid without objection in former and similar accounts; so, if it appear to be the invariable custom or usage in any particular trade or business to charge interest this may amount to evidence of an implied contract between parties to allow it in transactions therein.

It has been held that where a party is indebted to a trader who becomes bankrupt, in a sum bearing interest, the assignees may recover interest accruing subsequently to the bankruptcy, although there may appear to have been no *express* reservation of interest at all.

Discretion of Court in granting Interest. It will appear from this exposition of the law, which I have thought fit to state mostly in the words of a text-writer of authority, that before the statute of William IV. there were many cases of great hardship and injustice, where the jury could not give interest. It is left now to their *discretion* in these cases of "debt," or "sum certain." And also by another section of the Act they have power to give damages in the nature of interest in certain cases where the value of goods or chattels wrongfully taken, or detained, or applied, or "converted" by the defendant, is sought to be recovered. Where the legislature has left a question to the discretion of a jury or other tribunal representing it, I have no intention of attempting to lay down any rules which would fetter a Consular Court in the exercise of its discretion in particular cases. The circumstances under which claims have accrued, and are brought forward, their nature, the time

which has elapsed since the debt became due, and the reasons, or absence of reason, why the plaintiff has neglected to take means to recover it for any lengthened period: these and other points naturally come under the attention of the Court at the time of trial, and help it to a *just* order where that order is really discretionary,

There may be cases in which the custom of the particular place or particular business has removed the question of interest from the discretion of the Court, to the extent, at least, to which such custom is established, and where this is the case Consuls should, of course, act on the custom.

I now come to the consideration of damages in a more general sense, as compensation for a wrong done, in order that we may see on what principle they may be assessed. <small>Compensation by way of Damages.</small>

And, first, then, with regard to damages for a breach of contract, whether express or implied. There are, of course, many cases where the measure of damages for breach of contract will become apparent from the nature of the contract itself, unless where "consequential damages" are claimed, of which I shall presently speak. Work done at a price agreed on—goods sold and delivered at a stipulated price, give rise, when the price is not paid, to a demand on a promise to pay the sums respectively due, which are as certain as if they had been lent to the defendant. But if the work was done, or the goods supplied at the defendant's request, without any express stipulation as to price, inasmuch as the law would then imply a promise on his part to pay, the *value* of the labour or the goods would be the measure of the damages on non-payment, and must, if disputed, be ascertained. And I shall take this opportunity of observing that the general denial which, in Consular Courts, would be inferred from the absence of an answer, would not excuse the plaintiff from the proof of the value of the work or goods, nor ought the defendant to be precluded from showing that they were worthless, or of inferior quality, in order to reduce the damages.

Where the nature and circumstances of the contract, however, do not supply a direct or sure method of ascertaining the amount of damages, it does not unfrequently happen that in express written contracts the parties endeavour to supply this omission in contemplation of a breach by inserting a clause to the effect that the party making default shall pay to the other a certain sum of money, which sometimes is expressed to be by way of "penalty," sometimes as and for "liquidated" (that is, ascertained), damages for the breach. <small>Penalties on breaches of Contract.</small>

It is right to call the attention of those who have to administer justice, to the state of the law of England on clauses of this nature— and that with some degree of particularity, for it is in itself special, and founded on sometimes apparently fine, but very just, distinctions; and these provisions are not uncommon, under one form or another, in charter-parties, and very usual in other agreements, such as for building houses, &c.: matters which may come at any time before a Consul for his dicision. A case occurred at Constantinople before the establishment of the Supreme Court, in which a Mercantile Commission appointed by Her Majesty's Ambassador to assist him in an appeal from the decision of a Mixed Commission appear to have construed the words in a charter-party, "penalty for non-performance, so much," as giving the right to the plaintiff, on breach by the defendant, to recover the whole penal sum; and although they allowed the deduction of a small sum in consequence of certain absolute earnings by the ship, proved to have been received by the plaintiff, they gave a judgment for the residue, being the great bulk of the penal sum, without a thought apparently of calling on the plaintiff to prove what damage he had actually incurred. This judgment was put into execution, and I quote it as a specimen of the substantial injustice which the absence of knowledge, however natural and excusable, may inflict, and as a reason for calling special attention to the true difference between a penalty and liquidated damages.

Difference between "a Penalty" and "Liquidated damages." A penalty in the sense in which the law construes the word for the purpose of which I am speaking, is a sum intended to *cover* any damage which may be *actually incurred* by a breach of the contract.

"Liquidated damages" are the sum that is to be paid in the event of a breach, *without reference to the extent of the injury sustained.*

Now the first thing to be remarked is, that in a contract the use of the words, "as and for liquidated damages, and not by way of penalty," or words of a similar nature, are not *conclusive* of the real intention of the parties, which must be gathered from the whole instrument; and perhaps this is a safe rule, so far as it goes, "that where articles contain covenants for the performance of several things, *damages for the breach of any one of which are certain in their nature and amount,* and then one large sum is stated at the end to be paid upon breach of performance, that *must be considered as a penalty;* but where the damages in *every* case of breach would necessarily be uncertain in their nature and amount, then the sum may be considered as *stipulated or liquidated damages.* And where it is agreed that if a party do such a particular thing, such a sum shall be paid by him, there the sum stated may be treated as liquidated damages." Not conclusively, observe, that it *must;* but, as it is expressed elsewhere, where there is a provision that a certain sum shall be paid in the event of the performance or non-performance of a *particular specified* act with regard to which, in case of default, damages in their nature *uncertain* may arise, *and there are no words* evincing an intention *that the sum reserved shall be viewed as a penalty only,* then such sum may be recovered as liquidated damages.

The consideration of a few decided cases will make the foregoing observations more easy to understand.

In a case looked on until lately as the leading authority, the plaintiff and defendant agreed that the defendant should act in the plaintiff's theatre for four seasons, and should in all things conform to the regulations of the theatre; that the plaintiff should pay the defendant 3*l*. 8*s*. 6*d*. every night on which the theatre was open for theatrical performances; and that the defendant should be allowed a benefit, &c. And the agreement contained a clause, that if either of the parties should neglect or refuse to fulfil the said agreement, or any part thereof, or any stipulation therein contained, such party should pay to the other the sum of 1,000*l*., to which sum it was thereby agreed that the damages sustained by any such omission, neglect, or refusal should amount, and which sum was thereby declared by the said parties to be liquidated and ascertained damages,

and not a penalty or penal sum, or in the nature thereof.

On breach by the defendant, who refused to act during the second season, the Court of Common Pleas held the provision to be in the nature of a *penalty*, gathering the reasonable intention of the parties from the whole instrument; for, as was observed in the judgment, the clause was not confined to breaches which were of uncertain nature and amount (meaning apparently thereby breaches for which substantial damages, unascertained and difficult to ascertain, might be recoverable), but extended to *any* stipulations, so that if the plaintiff neglected to make one single payment of 3*l*. 8*s*. 6*d*., or the defendant omitted to conform to any regulation of the theatre however unimportant, the amount of 1,000*l*., without deduction, would instantly become due from one to the other, on the construction of the instrument, according to the letter of the words.

And it is certain that in these cases, whatever the language used, if it is plain from the whole instrument that the real intention of the parties was different, the Courts will not hold them to the language. If a sum be named in respect of the non-performance of one covenant only, and be expressly declared to be reserved as liquidated damages, and not as a penalty, it will be held to be the sole measure of damages between the parties; and were two persons agreed to perform certain work in a limited time, or to pay a stipulated weekly sum for such time afterwards as it should remain unfinished, the Court held that such weekly payments were not by way of penalty, but in the nature of liquidated damages.

Real intention of parties, the guide.

As an instance that the Courts do not regard the mere words, when inconsistent with the spirit and intention of the parties derived from the instrument itself, it may be mentioned that the very use of the word "penalty" in a stipulation of this kind will no more *conclude* the result, than the use of the words "liquidated damages." In a case where the agreement was that in consideration that the plaintiff, who was a surgeon, would engage the defendant as his assistant, the defendant promised not to practise within seven miles of the plaintiff's residence, under "a penalty" of 500*l*., it was held that, under this agreement, the 500*l*., though called a penalty, was recoverable as liquidated damages.

In a recent case the Court of Queen's Bench has expressed the principle of all the decisions to be, to ascertain what was the real intention of the parties as to the light in which the stipulated sum should be regarded, and that all rules laid down were only ancillary to the discovery of the intention. It may not be superfluous in quoting this, to point out that the "intention" is to be got from the instrument itself, and that it is not allowable to seek for evidence of it elsewhere. As to what rules are to guide the Court in judging of the intention, it is observed that the fact that the sum is large and exaggerated, does not *of itself* show that it was intended as a penalty. Again, the circumstance that more than one thing is to be done or forborne, does not determine the question. But the principle to be deduced from all the decisions is, that if the covenant relates to matters which are not of an uncertain nature and amount, as where the covenant is for the payment of a certain sum, and the damages named in the deed are a much larger sum, the sum so stated is to be regarded as a penalty. And if some of the stipulations in the covenant are of a certain nature and amount, and others of uncertain nature and amount, as the sum could not be treated as liquidated damages in respect of one or more of the stipulations, it ought not to be so treated in respect of the others. So, in another case, a distinguished Judge has laid down, that "if a party agrees to pay 1,000*l.* on several "events, all of which are capable of accurate valuation, the sum "must be construed as a penalty, and not as liquidated damages. "But if there be a contract, consisting of one or more stipulations, "the breach of which" (construed by another learned Judge to mean "all of which") "cannot be measured, then the parties must be taken "to have meant that the sum agreed on was to be taken as liquidated "damages, and not as a penalty."

The very common instance of "uncertain damage" in these cases is where a medical man on being brought into a partnership, covenants not to practise in a particular district after the dissolution of the partnership. If he breaks the covenant by attending a single case, it may be, as has been well said, the loss of a single bill, or it may lead to the loss of a line of practice, connection, fortune, of everything, in short, to the other party; and the Courts, in such a case, have always taken the sum stipulated, as "liquidated damages."

<small>When no damages are fixed.</small> In case the parties have not made any agreement for estimating the damages of a breach of contract, it becomes the duty of the Court to do so on the evidence adduced, whether by proof or admission. And first, it may be taken as a rule that the damages on a breach of contract to pay money, are, except so far as interest ought to be given, nominal; but in other cases, where an action is brought upon a contract for the recovery of general damages by reason of the non-performance of an act which the defendant had undertaken to perform, or the commission of an act which he had contracted to avoid, the Court may likewise take into consideration any consequential injury which the plaintiff has sustained, provided such injury be the fair and natural result of the defendant's violation of his agreement.

It is easy to perceive that in applying this rule, it may be often difficult to know how far to go; and I prefer giving some illustrations of the measure of damages recognized on argument by the Courts in certain ordinary cases, to quoting nice cases of difficulty which may illustrate the limits of the practice.

<small>Consequential damages.</small> Of contracts for money I have spoken, and I repeat that consequential damage for the non-payment of it according to the contract, is not allowed. This rule appears to be observed on motives of general convenience, for there is no saying what limit otherwise could be placed to the consequential damage arising from not paying money according to the promise; perhaps it is, on the whole, fair to calculate that the true damage is the interest at the current rate on the sum you are kept out of, for the time you are so kept out of it. However imperfect this measure of damages may be in certain cases, it is the one adopted.

In an action on breach of contract for not delivering goods upon a given day, the measure of damages is the difference between the contract price and that which goods of a similar quality and description bore in the market at the time the goods ought to have been

delivered; and this rule will hold good though the vendor had given notice before that day that he would not perform the contract (the buyer not agreeing, of course, to rescind), or though the buyer had, in pursuance of the contract, given bills of exchange for the goods; but in that case he must allow the bills to come to maturity and be dishonoured, as it would seem, before bringing his action.

The measure of damages in an action for not accepting railway shares, is the difference of the price of the shares in the market on the day when they ought to have been accepted, and on the day when they were resold by the vendor within a reasonable time.

It is said that in certain cases where the breach of contract is coupled with circumstances which place the defendant in the light of a wrong doer, the jury are allowed to take a greater latitude in assessing the damages; and in the familiar case of an action on breach of promise to marry, the jury are constantly in the habit of giving exemplary damages: nor will the Courts be disposed to interfere, except in case of very excessive damages.

There is a rule with regard to special damage in English pleading, *Special damage.* of which the principle is so sound that ought to be enforced in petitions in Consular Courts. It may be laid down thus, as applicable here, that damages which necessarily and by implication of law arise from the non-performance of a contract, need not be expressly stated, although they must be included in the calculation of the sum claimed for damages in the petition, inasmuch as the plaintiff cannot possibly recover more; but if any part of the sum laid as damages consists, in the plaintiff's calculation, of damages special or consequential under particular circumstances, and not such as the law would always imply, he should set out his special damage expressly; for the defendant is entitled to know in respect of what facts he claims such damages, so that he may be prepared to rebut the facts, or argue that the consequence is *too remote*, in the general contemplation of law, to enable the plaintiff to recover that part of his claim.

In actions which in England are classed under the general head *Damages in Actions of "Tort."* of "torts" (a term used to signify such *wrongs* as are in their nature distinguishable from breaches of contract), the measure of damages differs very materially in practice. In some, as in "trover," where the value of goods of the plaintiff supposed to be converted by the defendant to his own use is sought for, the proper measure of damages would be the value and reasonable consequential damage for their "conversion" or loss to the plaintiff.

Under one section of the Act I have alluded to, the jury may give interest on the sum assessed as the value for the detention. In the action of "detinue," where the judgment is that the plaintiff recover the specific thing, or its value, assessed at so much, with damages for its detention, a jury in England has been permitted to give a very high value, for the purpose of ensuring the return of the chattel; for a Court of Law had no power to compel the specific delivery up of the thing in dispute; but the jurisdiction of the Consular Courts, which enables them, when the chattel in dispute can and ought to be delivered up by the defendant, to compel him to do so, renders it unnecessary in most intances to resort to such means.

In many instances, however, of actions of this large class, the discretion of the jury is not only practically unfettered at the time, but the Courts will not grant new trials for excess of damages, except in gross cases, where the damages given are absurd in amount, showing unjustifiable passion or prejudice on the part of the jury; or where the jury seem clearly to have taken a wrong view, through ignorance of the principle on which they ought to act.

Exemplary damages. In actions for libel, seduction, assault, false imprisonment, malicious prosecution or arrest, and the like, the jury are allowed, in practice, to grant heavy damages, although no special damage may be established. I am happy to say that proceedings of this kind have, in my experience here, been very rare, possibly from the absence of profitable costs; and it is only necessary to repeat on this subject the warning given generally to juries in these cases to be *temperate* in assessing damages in actions of this description. Actions for mere slander are discouraged, unless the plaintiff can show special damage caused by the slanderous words.

Excessive damages, ground of Appeal. To grant excessive, that is, clearly unreasonable damages, is to lay a ground for an appeal; and in cases where a sum certain is demanded and should have been granted, to grant a less sum would also lay open the judgment to objection. It will be well, where Consuls think that there is an *arguable* ground of objection to their judgment, in either of these respects, to reserve leave for an application to the Supreme Court, on the record and notes of evidence, to reduce or increase the damages, the Court being at liberty to draw inferences of fact from the evidence, as if it were a jury; and this may often save the expense of a new trial. This necessity may fairly be expected to arise not unfrequently in those cases where remoteness of consequential damage allowed is the ground of objection to the judgment; in such cases the party objecting to the judgment on other grounds also, may, of course, appeal generally, so that the Court would be able to consider the two points in succession, and do justice by one order.

Bankruptcy. A Bankruptcy jurisdiction in Consular Courts is now recognized and authorized by the Order in Council. It is one of importance and delicacy; and it is necessary that as much uniformity as possible should be observed in its exercise.

The number of bankruptcies is very considerable, while the cases very seldom indeed go through their ordinary course.

They are almost invariably commenced by an adjudication on the petition of the person seeking to become bankrupt, with the object to save himself from arrest, or defeat some particular judgment creditor. And the want of knowledge of the law, and the absence of persons accustomed to sift out the truth in public examinations, too often enable the debtor to conceal (even if he takes the trouble to conceal) and enjoy valuable assets which ought of right to have gone to his creditors.

The Rules do not contain provisions specially applicable to Bankruptcy, partly because the Acts of Parliament now in force in England and the Rules made under them appear to be at present for most purposes a sufficient guide, and partly because extensive and important changes, both in principle and in detail, are expected to be soon introduced into the system in England.

Every Consul acting in these matters ought to possesses a good edition of the Acts for the time being in force, with a compendious statement of the usual steps in a bankruptcy in their course and order, and containing notes showing how incidental questions have been decided, and what are the principles established for the decision of others likely to arise.

I cannot pretend, in a circular of this kind, to supply a substitute for such a guide; but it may not be useless to point out the general principles and chief details of the existing system, a knowledge of which will, moreover, be the best assistant to the Consul when it becomes his duty to acquaint himself with the new principles and practice which, as I have said, are likely to be before long introduced in this department of the law.

In all cases of doubt or difficulty the Consul should remember that he is at liberty to apply to the Supreme Court for advice and direction.

The English bankruptcy laws as they now exist may be properly said to have a double object—to enforce complete discovery and equitable distribution of the property and effects of an insolvent; and to secure to him, as an equivalent the discharge from his liabilities, both in person, and in after-acquired property. Provision is made to suspend, or even altogether to refuse this discharge, where the conduct of the insolvent prevents his creditors from having the benefit of the intention of the law, whether by his faults of omission or commission. And he is either perpetually disabled (unless after full satisfaction of his debts) from trading or acquiring property to his own profit; or his right to do so is suspended for a definite time, either with or without personal protection against arrest by his creditors: so that he returns to trade, freed, indeed, from his debts, but with such a mark against him as a dishonest or reckless trader, as must seriously impair his credit, and bar his prospects. *Object of Bankrupt Law.*

The provisions of the laws of bankruptcy are generally well adapted to discover and punish dishonesty, and to protect mere misfortune; any person is liable to be adjudicated bankrupt, on the commission of an act of bankruptcy.

Acts of bankruptcy may be divided into two classes, the fomer of which have all one necessary element involved in them, namely, that they must be done with intent to defeat or delay the creditors; the latter class are independent of intention, but one of them consists in a declaration of insolvency; and another, which consists in remaining in prison for a certain time under arrest for debt, or other process for the non-payment of money, raises an irresistible presumption to the same effect. The escape from confinement on civil process, is also, in itself, an act of bankruptcy, and this is probably based on a similar presumption of insolvency. *Acts of Bankruptcy.*

The application for adjudication is seldom hostile here; indeed, the filing of a petition of adjudication by the debtor against himself, is by far the most common commencement of the proceedings. However, it is proper to consider first the method by which one person can obtain an adjudication of bankruptcy against another. A form of petition and of the accompanying affidavit is given by the Act of Parliament, and the necessary particulars which must be *Petition for adjudication.*

sworn to, and of which the Court must be satisfied before the adjudication, are specified.

The petitioner, it will be seen, must be a creditor, and that to the extent of 50l.

Must be in respect of a Debt.

The debt must be a debt in the strict sense, and actually due and payable.

And the person petitioned against must have committed some act of bankruptcy.

Joint Petition.

There are provisions with regard to the case of a joint petition by creditors, to which it is not necessary more specially to refer; the principle will be apparent. No one but a creditor to a substantial amount ought to be enabled to compel a trader to wind up his affairs in bankruptcy; but if several persons having debts owing to them, each within the limit arbitrarily prescribed, but amounting in the whole to a large and substantial liability, are all desirous of having the debtor's affairs investigated and his property divided in Bankruptcy, they are at liberty to do so. It will be observed also, that the Act allows any creditor who could have himself supported a petition for adjudication, to take up and proceed upon one which may have been abandoned, thus endeavouring to prevent collusion and undue preference.

Any debtor may petition for adjudication of Bankruptcy against himself and the filing of such a petition is itself an act of Bankruptcy. A debtor imprisoned for debt, and unable through the expenses attending the points to pay for the filing of a petition may petition *in formâ pauperis*.

Adjudication.

If the Court, on the hearing of the petition of adjudication is satisfied that the requirements of the law have been complied with, it is bound to adjudicate, and, on adjudication, certain notices become necessary, which naturally lead me to say something as to the manner in which the act of Parliament is to be complied with, and the extent to which it is necessary to carry out its provisions to the latter. And first, it is clear that there are directions as to advertising, and the like, which in some cases are impossible, in others, useless. It is not impossible, but useless, to advertise an adjudication of bankruptcy against a merchant at Shanghai or Yokohama in the "London Gazette;" it is however quite possible to do so in a local paper where one exists. The object, must be to comply with the spirit of the Act as to public announcements in the most public way that is available; and with regard to all notices, wherein a certain number of days are prescribed, this should be executed to the letter, for, in these instances, spirit and letter are one. So in those cases where officers of the Court of Bankruptcy in England are mentioned in the Act, which do not exist in most, if in any, Consular Courts. The spirit of the Act is complied with when the terms are taken to apply to those who are performing the functions and duties appertaining to their respective offices. Now, after adjudication has been pronounced, the English law, mindful that such a proceeding must often take place, *ex parte*, and anxious that a fatal blow may not be given to the public credit of a trader who may really be solvent, notwithstanding that he has committed the particular act of bankruptcy, delays for a certain number of days

the advertisement of adjudication, unless the bankrupt expressly consents to an earlier advertisement. It is clearly the duty of the Consular Court to carry into effect this provision, whatever meaning it may have to attach to the word "advertisement," so that the bankrupt may have the full benefit of the opportunity allowed to come in, and either dispute the adjudication, or settle with the creditor, which, if he is really solvent, it is most just that he should be permitted to do so.

The essential duties which are to be performed after adjudication, for the purpose of making it answer its intended purposes, consist in giving notice of it to the public, so that no person may pay money or deliver goods to, or receive them from the bankrupt; also, in taking possession of all existing goods belonging to the bankrupt; and, moreover, in appointing certain days upon which he is to surrender, personally, for the purpose of being examined, touching his estate and effects, and being dealt with generally, according to the provisions of the Bankrupt Laws. This surrender is always looked on as a matter of the highest possible importance, for the creditors are entitled to the bankrupt's information and assistance in the winding-up and recovery of his estate; and if *they are not*, at least the Court *is* entitled to have personal control over him, so that, if he has acted fraudulently or recklessly, he may be at hand to meet the consequences of his acts. No discharge can accordingly be granted unless the bankrupt surrenders; but, in addition to this, he incurs a far heavier penalty by not surrendering, being thereby, *ipso facto*, guilty of a misdemeanour, and liable to imprisonment for three years. *Proceedings after Adjudication.*

No Consul should ordinarily allow criminal proceedings to be taken against any person for an offence against the bankrupt laws without first applying for advice and instructions to the Supreme Court; and I trust that the whole jurisdiction is now settled on so clear a footing as to enable this Court to take effective steps for the punishment of fraudulent bankrupts, with a due regard to that security which the whole spirit of the English law throws round persons who are not really guilty. In no one point is the superiority of our system more apparent over that of the foreign codes than in all proceedings relating to bankruptcy when carried on in these countries. *Criminal proceedings under Bankrupt Law.*

It is, I have no hesitation in saying, almost impossible for foreign trader, however honest his general dealings may have been, to escape the danger of incurring a severe penal liability under the unbending provisions of most foreign codes, under which, in such countries as China and Japan, every "faillite," if narrowly scrutinised, is pretty sure to turn into a "culpable" or "fraudulent bancarotta." The English system, far more elastic in its provisions, keeps the power in the hands of those who have to administer it, of discriminating between every grade of imprudence up to that degree of reckless trading which amounts to positive fraud, and of awarding to each separate case a retribution adequate and appropriate. In practice, as might have been expected, the system of the code has defeated itself. And what between a want of will on the part of creditors, and a want of power in the Consular Courts, fraudulent bankruptcies of a very gross kind have taken place with perfect impunity. I know of no one instance of punishment, nor is it at all to be expected until creditors become more alive to their interests and duties that the criminal sections of the bankrupt act are likely to be productive of benefit. Either fraudulent bankrupts must escape for want of evidence, or be convicted on materials which, according to our notions and principles, would be grossly insufficient. And such convictions we generally suppose to produce more harm than good. Indeed, example on the spot is what is wanted, and that under such clear circumstances as will ensure the assent of the whole mercantile communities to the conviction and punishment.

It will be observed that one of the first duties after an adjudication in bankruptcy, imposed on the Court, is to name an official assignee, and in some shape, and for some purposes, it is desirable that an officer attached to the Consulate, or some solvent and respectable person, not a creditor, should fill this office.

Securing Estate of Bankrupt. — In the first place, it is requisite to give directions for securing the bankrupt's estate, and looking into his affairs immediately; and before trade assignees are appointed by the creditors, much time may be lost and irreparable mischief done. The person so appointed, should, forthwith, under the leave and direction of the Court, secure the bankrupt's property, ascertain that he is forthcoming, and not likely to abscond; and require from him a list of the creditors, a list of the debtors to the estate, a statement of rent (if any) due on premises occupied by him, and of wages due to servants or clerks, a statement of the probable value of the stock-in-trade, furniture, &c., and a list of the books, papers, securities, and the like, verified on oath. These books and papers ought to be the object of special and immediate attention, and some provision ought to be made for their safe custody, care being taken at the same time that the bankrupt can have convenient access to them from time to time. I am of opinion that all payment received on account of the estate should be immediately deposited in the Consulate, and entered in the deposit account to the credit of the particular estate in bankruptcy. The official assignee ought to direct the payment of moneys due to the bankrupt's estate into the Consulate, probably in all cases, and take a note from time to time of what has been so paid; it will be his duty to enforce (with leave of the Court first obtained) the payment of sums due and remaining unpaid; and, in short, to perform singly, until the appointment of the creditor's assignees, all necessary acts for the realization and safe custody of the estate, and for the proper investigation of the accounts. He should also be at liberty to apply for and obtain permission of the Court to pay such small debts out of the estate as from their nature must be paid, and which ought to be paid immediately, and to take care that no unnecessary liability is incurred as to warehouses or other establishments.

Official Assignee. — The person acting as official assignee ought to be essentially for that purpose an officer of the Court, alike independent of the bankrupt and his creditors, and conversant with business and accounts. The Court relies on him in a great measure for an impartial account of the conduct of the bankrupt, with respect to the realization of his estate, and explanation of his dealings; although, of course, in this

and in all other matters, the creditors assignees are able to exercise an efficient check over any undue partiality or other abuse of the confidence reposed in this officer.

It is not probable that it will be at all necessary to separate the duties of the official assignee in bankruptcy from the Consular Officer of the place. In most cases the instances of bankruptcy are not numerous enough, nor other judicial business sufficiently heavy, to prevent Chief Assistant or Vice-Consul from seeing to those points which lie within the province of an official assignee: and the practical limitation of the jurisdiction in bankruptcy in all cases of amount and importance by a reference of them to the Supreme Court removes the objection which might otherwise be raised to the performance of these duties by the person who under the present system, has to act in some respects as a Commissioner.

After the appointment of the official assignee, and before advertisement of the adjudication, and at or before the time of putting in execution any warrant of seizure granted on such adjudication, a duplicate of the adjudication is to be served on the person adjudged bankrupt, *personally*, or by leaving the same as directed by the Act at his last known place of business or abode. And such person is to be allowed *seven* days, or any extended time not exceeding *fourteen* days, from service, to show cause against the adjudication. If he does so, he is to give previous notice of what particular thing he intends to dispute, whether the petitioning creditor's debt, the trading, or the act of bankruptcy; and on the day fixed for showing cause the particular part of the proceeding which it is intended to dispute must be again proved by *vivâ voce* evidence, unless otherwise specially directed; and if new matter arises, or witnesses are not present to be cross-examined, the Court may grant further time to show cause. Service of adjudication.

If, on showing cause, the petitioning creditor's debt, the act of bankruptcy, or any or either of such matters, are or is shown to be insufficient to support the adjudication, and no other sufficient matter to supply the place of the particular thing which is shown to be insufficient, is proved, then the adjudication is to be annulled.

If no sufficient cause is shown, the Court is to appoint a public meeting for the bankrupt to surrender.

Any steps to annul the adjudication taken *after* the *fourteen* days, should be in every instance taken before the Supreme Court: the particular Consul having jurisdiction in Bankruptcy corresponding in this respect to the Commissioner who has no power to entertain a proceeding to annul adjudication commenced after the expiration of that time. Annulling adjudication.

The bankrupt may surrender at any time after notice of adjudication, and within the time limited. He does so by merely appearing before the Court, and signing a memorandum to that effect. Surrender of Bankrupt.

At this first meeting, of which ten days notice must be given, proof of debts are received. The official assignee gives the fullest information in his power of the estate and effects of the bankrupt, and the majority in value of creditors present may if they please assent to an allowance being made to the bankrupt until the first examination. At this meeting creditor's assignees may be chosen. First Meeting.

Second Meeting. The first meeting of creditors being concluded a day is appointed for a second sitting, when the bankrupt is to pass his final examination. He is then and there to disclose the whole of the property, and to account for the manner in which any part of it has been disposed of. The spirit and substance of the provisions in the Act which require the preparation and filing of a balance-sheet, ought to be fully carried into execution. And in no case should the last examination of the bankrupt be passed by the Court, unless the balance-sheet has been duly filed. Adjournments of the meeting, if necessary, for the amendment of the balance-sheet may be allowed, or the meeting may be adjourned *sine die*, if the balance-sheet and bankrupt's answers are unsatisfactory. It is the open examination of the bankrupt by his creditors and the Court on the last examination, which affords the best security for the discovery of improper conduct; and the penalty which a bankrupt incurs under the 221st section of the Bankruptcy Act 1861 for not disclosing or embezzling and part of his estate is enough to deter most from such malpractices.

Power of Court to summon any Person. But besides this, the Court is invested with a power of summoning before it, at any time after adjudication, persons suspected to have any part of the bankrupt's estate in their possession or supposed to be indebted to him, or capable of giving information as to the person, trade, dealings, or estate of the bankrupt, and may require them to produce books and papers, and may examine them on oath, forcing them to subscribe their answers when reduced into writing.

Court may examine Bankrupt's wife. And the Court may further summon and examine, on statutory declaration, the bankrupt either before or after he has received his certificate, and may summon and in like manner examine his wife, for the full discovery of the property of the bankrupt.

Search Warrants. Also search warrants may be granted, after evidence on oath has made it appear, to the satisfaction of the Court, that there is reason to suspect and believe that any part of the bankrupt's property is concealed in any house or premises not belonging to the bankrupt, or for the purpose of securing the person of the bankrupt himself, if in concealment. In short, by the Statute Law of England, the most extensive powers are given for the benefit of the estate to the Commissioners; but in exercising their jurisdiction in bankruptcy, Consuls will do well to remain strictly within the limits of the jurisdiction conferred upon them, however desirable the exercise of power in a doubtful case might appear in any particular instance.

Letters to Bankrupt. It will be seen, however, by the nature of the provisions of the statute, what immense importance is attached to the object of facilitating the getting hold of the bankrupt's estate, and preventing fraudulent concealment: indeed the Court in England may order the Postmaster-General to cause all letters directed to the bankrupt to be re-directed to the assignees for a certain time, and may renew such order from time to time.

All Bankrupt's Estate vests in assignees. The 141st section of the Act of 1849, provides for the vesting of the personal estate and effects of, and of the rights and interest in, debts owing to the bankrupt, in the assignees for the time being, for the benefit of the creditors.

Assignees of Bankrupt. The assignees are entitled to all rights of action which the bank-

rupt had, or which may accrue to him, until he shall have obtained his certificate, in respect of his property, and may sue upon them in their own name, in their representative character.

I have already stated, that where an official assignee is appointed, it is done immediately after adjudication.

The Act provides for the choice of creditors' assignees at the first public sitting after adjudication, or at some adjournment thereof. And they are elected by the major part in value of the creditors who shall have proved debts, voting at the meeting; Persons holding powers of attorney from creditors so qualified are also entitled to vote, on proof of the execution thereof, either by affidavit or on *vivâ voce* evidence; but the Court has a power to reject any person so chosen as assignee, and also to remove any assignee for unfitness. They are subject to the order of the Court in their conduct as assignees. Up to the time of their appointment, the estate and effects of the bankrupt are vested in the official assignee, but on their appointment the property then vests in them, and is divested out of the official assignee. Power to remove assignees.

Although it is said that they need not necessarily be creditors, yet in all cases it is desirable that they should be so, as it is obvious that their own interest will make them more active in realizing and distributing the bankrupt's estate.

Actions and suits are to be prosecuted and defended by them, with leave of the Court, and they may, with like leave and after such notices to creditors, or with such consent of creditors, or a proportion thereof, as the Court may direct, give time, or accept security, or compound for debts due to the bankrupt, and may refer matters relating to the estate to arbitration. Actions by and against assignees

There are other special provisions on these subjects, to which it is not necessary to refer at greater length; but it is right to remark that the assignees are not bound to adopt the bankrupt's contracts, and if they do *not* they are not subject to any action in respect of them. Thus, if the bankrupt have purchased land or goods, the assignees *may adopt* the purchase, if they will; and if they do, they become liable, but if they do not they are *not* so liable.

Questions involving the assignees in litigation frequently arise, under the 125th section of the Act of 1849 of which it is necessary to speak a little in detail.

If any bankrupt at the time he becomes bankrupt (*i. e.* commits the act of bankruptcy upon which the adjudication proceeds), shall by the consent and permission of the true owner thereof, have in his possession, order, or disposition, any goods or chattels whereof he was reputed owner, or whereof he had taken upon him the sale, alteration, or disposition as owner, the Court shall have power to order the same to be sold and disposed of for the benefit of the creditors. (There is an exception for registered mortgages and assignments of ships, under the Acts relating to British vessels.) Goods in order and disposition of Bankrupt.

The object of this provision is obviously to protect creditors who may have been supposed to have given credit to the bankrupt, upon the faith of the apparent property which he had in the goods in question, and the numerous cases have proceeded, although not always consistently, on this principle. It is obvious that the question always involves one of fact: namely, the consent and permission of the true owner, which may be negatived by proof of any previous order or request to the bankrupt by the owner to deliver up the goods. In order that the creditors may have the benefit of such property, there must be an order of the Court to sell and dispose of it, and the validity of that order depends upon the fact I have just referred to.

It has been held, that where the goods were in the order and disposition of a trader, at the time he committed an act of bankruptcy, but were taken out of his possession by the true owner after the act of bankruptcy, but before the petition, and without notice of an act of bankruptcy, they could not be ordered to be sold by the assignees; and this under the 133rd section of the Act of 1849 for the protection of *bonâ fide* transactions, without notice of any previous act of bankruptcy.

Assignees may recover possession of Bankrupt's property.
The assignees may recover the bankrupt's property in the possession of any agent, satisfying any lien, and may perform conditions, or tender payment of money, where necessary, for the recovery of property pledged or mortgaged; and they are often obliged to take proceedings to recover property conveyed or assigned without valuable consideration, or by way of fraudulent preference, as where a trader, in contemplation of bankruptcy, voluntarily assigns or transfers some of his property to one of his creditors, with intent to give him a preference, such an assignment is not only void,—the very object and essence of the bankrupt laws being to insure a fair and equal distribution of the estate,—but it is also an act of bankruptcy. These cases also involve questions of fact, which bring the assignees, as plaintiffs, before the Courts of Law, and it is their duty to proceed, where practicable, and where it is likely to prove advantageous to the estate.

Sales by Auction.
In realizing the estate, it is usual to sell the property by auction, and I see no reason here to depart from this practice. In the meanwhile, the debts are to be collected, and payment enforced, if necessary, and the whole of the money paid into Court. Payment to the assignees by a debtor of the estate, under a judgment or decree, is a discharge, although the adjudication be annulled. And even without action or suit, *bonâ fide* delivery of goods, or payment of money, claimed by assignees, is a discharge as against the bankrupt, and persons claiming under him, unless the persons so paying or delivering goods had notice of some action, suit, or other proceeding, to dispute or annul the petition or adjudication. And so much for the collection and realization of the estate, and the method adopted under our law to ascertain its extent, and to secure it, to which ends the surrender and examination of the bankrupt principally tend.

Proof of Debts.
It now remains for me to say something, in equally general terms, as to the proof of debts under the bankruptcy, the rights of creditors, the discharge, its effect, and the consequences of its suspension or refusal.

What debts to be paid in full.
There are certain debts which must be either paid in full, or of which a greater part is payable than would come to the creditor under an ordinary dividend. Thus clerks and servants of the bankrupt are entitled to receive their respective salaries and wages in full, for three months, if so much is due, to an extent not exceeding 30*l*.:

they must prove for the residue, if any. A labourer, or workman, is entitled to his wages out of the estate to the extent of 40s., and may prove for any balance. And inasmuch as an adjudication operates as a discharge of the indenture of an apprentice to the bankrupt, the Court may order out of the estate the return of so much of any apprentice-fee, or premium, actually paid, as it thinks fit, having regard to the length of time the apprentice shall have resided with the bankrupt previous to the filing of the petition. *Apprentices.*

The English law allows a landlord to satisfy a distress for rent, made after an act of bankruptcy, to the extent of one year's rent only; for the residue, if any, which may be in arrear, he must prove with the other creditors. In these countries, it would seem at first sight that these provisions could only be strictly enforced where the landlord, as well as the tenant, is a British subject; but as rent is mostly payable in advance, practical inconveniences will probably be of rare occurrence, and where application is made to the Court by a foreign landlord to sequester goods of an adjudicated bankrupt for rent in arrear, I see no objection or difficulty in following the course of English law, and in practice, this is the only form in which a landlord does seize goods. *Rent.*

The 164th section of the Act of 1849 and the 144th of that of 1861, give directions for the time and manner of the proof of debts, and the first thing to remark is, that the proof is admitted and recorded at a public sitting, where all creditors have a right to be present, and both they and the assignees may oppose any proof. It is, of course, the interest of creditors to admit as few people to share in the dividend as possible, and they as well as the Court are enabled to see the nature of any claim, proof of which is tendered; but the Court decides whether to admit, or reject, or adjourn the proof, and it does this on some evidence, the mere admission by the bankrupt not being in itself sufficient. In practice, it is customary for creditors to show the nature of their claim beforehand to the assignees, or, at least, to the official assignee, and in clear cases the Court will, in the absence of opposition, admit the proof, on the oath or legal affirmation of the creditor, or on an affidavit by him. *Creditors and assignees may oppose proof of debts.*

All causes of action for which, if payable, the original party might maintain the action of debt, whether on simple contract, deed, or judgment, may be proved either by the party himself, or by any person to whom he has assigned them; and judgment creditors may prove for their costs. Interest on debts may also be proved for, at the rate of 4 per cent. per annum, under circumstances in which, by 3 & 4 Wm. IV. cap. 42, sec. 28, interest might have been awarded in an action. That provision has been discussed in an earlier part of this circular letter. *What debts proveable.*

A creditor may prove for any amount for which he has given credit on valuable consideration, whether such credit shall or shall not have been given upon any bill, bond, note, or other negotiable security, although the debt be not payable at the time of the act of bankruptcy; and such creditor may receive dividends, allowing only a rebate for interest at 5 per cent., from the time of declaration of dividend to that at which, by the contract, the debt would have been payable. Obligees in bottomry and respondentia bonds, and assured in policies of insurance, may claim, and, after loss or contingency, prove and receive dividends. Annuity creditors may prove for the value of the annuity at the time of the petition for adjudication, and sureties for the payment of annuities may discharge themselves by paying the amount so proved, and shall thereupon stand in the place of the annuitant as creditors in the bankruptcy. There are special provisions with regard to the sureties or persons otherwise liable for debts of the bankrupt, and persons who have become bail for him in civil actions, the gist of which is, that they may prove for whatever they have paid in respect of their obligations, and the act of bankruptcy does not affect their rights, unless they had notice of it, or of some other act of bankruptcy, at the time they became surety or bail, or made themselves otherwise liable. In like manner, persons with whom the bankrupt shall have really, and *bonâ fide*, contracted debts prior to the petition for adjudication, shall be admitted to prove them, notwithstanding that such debts may have been contracted since the commission of any act of bankruptcy, so as the creditor shall not at the time have had notice of any act of bankruptcy on the part of the bankrupt.

Debts payable on a contingency. Debts payable on a contingency which shall not have happened prior to the petition shall, if the creditor desire it, be valued, and he may prove for such value; or, if the value be not ascertained before the happening of the contingency, he may, when the contingency has happened, prove for the whole debt, and receive dividends, not disturbing former dividends. An instance of a contingent debt is supplied by the case of a bankrupt who has been guarantee for another for a sum certain: when the guarantee is due, it is proveable as a debt, payable on a contingency. It is clear that to bring a debt payable on a contingency within the provisions of the former part of this section the contingency must be reducible to calculation, so as to admit of valuation of the present worth of the debt; and a section of the Act provides for the case where a bankrupt has contracted a liability to pay money on a contingency which shall not have happened, and the demand in respect thereof shall not have been ascertained before the filing of the petition. The person with whom the liability was contracted may claim for such sum as the Court shall think fit; and when the contingency happens, and the demand is ascertained, may convert his claim into a proof, receiving dividends, without disturbing former dividends; but if the claim shall not, within six months after petition for adjudication, be converted, either in whole or in part, into a proof, the Court may, on application by the assignees, expunge it, either in whole or in part, from the proceedings.

Agents. The 179th section of the Act of 1849 deserves a little special consideration, referring, as it does to the provisions of another Act of Parliament (5 & 6 Vict., cap. 39), under which cases may be of frequent occurrence in China and Japan. By the last-mentioned Act, any agent entrusted with the possession of goods, or of the documents of title to goods, shall be deemed the owner of such goods and documents, so far as to give validity to any contract or agreement by way of pledge, lien, or security, *bonâ fide* made by any person with such agent so entrusted as aforesaid, as well for any original loan,

advance, or payment made upon the security of such goods or documents, as also for any further or continuing advance in respect thereof; and such contracts shall be binding against the owner and all persons interested therein, notwithstanding the person claiming such pledge or lien may have had notice that the person with whom such contract or agreement is made is only an agent; and any bill of lading, India warrant, dock-warrant, warehouse-keeper's certificate, warrant or order for the delivery of goods, or any other document used in the ordinary course of business as proof of the possession or control of goods, or authorising, or purporting to authorise, either by indorsement or delivery, the possessor of such document to transfer or receive goods thereby represented, shall be deemed a document of title within the Act. There is also provision made for the right of the owner to redeem the goods or documents, on payment of the amount for which they are pledged, and on satisfaction of any lien which the agent who pledged them might legally set up, either against the goods or documents, or against the produce of their sale in the hands of the person to whom they stand pledged, after satisfaction of such pledge.

Now the 179th section of the Act of 1849 provides, that on the bankruptcy of the agent in any such case, the owner, if he has redeemed the goods, shall, in respect of the sum paid by him on account of the agent for redemption, be held to have paid such sum for the use of such agent; or, in case the goods shall not be redeemed, the owner shall be deemed a creditor of the agent to the value of the goods so pledged at the time of the pledge, and shall, in either of such cases, be entitled, if he shall think fit, to prove for or set off the sum so paid, or the value of such goods, as the case may be.

It is provided by the 171st section, that where there has been mutual credit given by the bankrupt and any other person, or where there are mutual debts between the bankrupt and any other person, the Court shall state the account between them, and one debt or demand may be set against another, notwithstanding prior acts of bankruptcy. And what shall appear due on either side on the balance of such account, and no more, shall be claimed or paid on either side respectively; and debts and demands made proveable under the Act may also be set off, in manner aforesaid, against the estate, if the person claiming the benefit of the set-off had not, when credit was given, notice of an act of bankruptcy. *Mutual credits or debts.*

It is to be observed that the provision with respect to mutual credits is confined to debts between the bankrupt and other parties, or to transactions necessarily ending in debts; but it has been held that the relation contemplated by the statute is established where the debt is immediately due from one party, and only due at a future time from the other, provided there is no uncertainty that the party said to receive the credit will become, sooner or later, debtor to the other.

Mortgagees, or other persons having security over any part of the bankrupt's estate or effects, may apply to the Court, if they think fit, but they are not bound to do so. If they do apply the Court is to inquire into the fact and nature of consideration for the security, and the circumstances under which it was given; and if the party *Mortgagees.*

claiming appears entitled to the security and to the sum claimed under it, shall take an account of what is due for principal, interest, and costs, setting off anything received in respect thereof. And the Court is to give notice and sell the property, the assignees having the conduct of the sale. Proper parties are to join in the transfer, as the Court shall direct, and the money is to be employed, first, in payment of the costs and expenses of the assignees in the application to the Court and the sale, and then in payment to the person holding the security of what has been found due for principal, interest, and costs.

The creditor may prove for the deficiency, if any, and receive dividends, not disturbing former ones: and if there shall, on the other hand, be any surplus it goes, of course, to the assignees for the benefit of the estate. Plenary powers are given to the Court for the purpose of ensuring a good sale by making a good title, to call all parties before it and examine them, making them produce books, papers, and deeds.

I cannot help thinking that a discreet use and application of these particular provisions would sometimes be of great service in assisting *bonâ fide* holders of securities, or persons who have advanced money on title deeds to land or houses in these countries to realize fairly; but, of course, numerous instances must occur, where the conflict of different jurisdictions will prevent the benefit of the law.

It is to be observed that the application by the mortgagee, or other person holding security, is not imperative on him: he may, if he pleases, stand upon his security, and if he have an absolute power of sale, such as is found in many mortgages, he will need the assistance neither of the bankruptcy Court or the Court of Chancery to enable him to foreclose: but if he wishes to prove, he must give up or realize his security under the direction of the Court. An attachment, or, as here, a sequester, is such a security, and it either must be given up or realized for the benefit of the estate, if the creditor wishes to prove for his whole debt. If he has realized by execution, seizure and sale, any part of his security before the filing of the petition for adjudication, he is at liberty to prove for any balance remaining due; but if he desires to prove for the whole debt, he must surrender what he has so realized, and after the filing of the petition he cannot realize his security except under the provisions I have before alluded to, without giving up his right to prove, for the bankrupt laws go upon the principle, as far as possible, of putting all creditors on an equal footing.

Note, however, that if the creditor has security for his debt on the estate of *a third person*, he may prove under the bankruptcy, without surrendering that, for the whole amount of his debt, and receive dividends, provided that, on the whole, he does not by any means whatsoever receive more than twenty shillings in the pound.

There are two sets of cases of frequent occurrence, which require mention.

If a partner of a firm be separately adjudicated bankrupt, the *creditors of the firm* are entitled to prove against the estate for the purpose of voting in the choice of assignees, and of being heard against his certificate; but they are not entitled to any dividend

until all the separate creditors have received their debts in full. But the separate creditor of any bankrupt is at liberty to prove his debt under any adjudication of bankruptcy made against such bankrupt jointly with any other person or persons, and the separate and joint estates are to be kept distinct, and the separate creditors satisfied, in the first place, out of the separate estates, and in case there is an overplus of the separate estates, it is to be carried to the account of the joint estate, and in case there is an overplus of the joint estates, it is to be carried to the account of the separate estates of each bankrupt, in proportion to the right and interest of each bankrupt in the joint estate.

The 97th section of the Act of 1849 has provided that any creditor whose debt is sufficient to entitle him to petition for adjudication of bankruptcy against all the partners of any firm, may petition for such adjudication against one or more partners of such firm; and every such petition shall be valid, though it does not include all the partners; and in every such petition against two or more persons, the Court may dismiss the same as to one or more of such persons, and the validity of such petition shall not be thereby invalidated as to any person as to whom such petition is not ordered to be dismissed, nor shall any such person's certificate be thereby affected.

The 98th section has also made provision for the case where, after a petition for adjudication against or by any one or more partners, any other petition for adjudication against or by any other member or members of the same firm shall be filed. It shall be prosecuted in the same Court, the property of the bankruptcy under the second adjudication shall vest in the assignees of the first bankruptcy, and the proceedings in the second shall, without affecting the validity of the first petition, be annexed to and form part of the proceedings in first, subject to special directions on the subject, which, in China and Japan must be obtained from the Supreme Court. I refer to the latter section, as involving an important principle of procedure, in order to avoid the expensive and possibly conflicting proceedings under two adjudications where the subject-matter would, in fact, be one.

An appeal is given from a proof, and also from a decision expunging a proof. <small>Appeal.</small>

It has been held in England that if a bankrupt applies to expunge a proof, he ought to allege and prove the probability of a surplus, or of his being entitled to an allowance, in short, to show an interest in the question which he desires to raise.

It will be seen, subsequently, that all debts and demands proveable under the bankruptcy are absolutely barred by the certificate; but provision is made for the case where a creditor has brought an action, or instituted a suit against the bankrupt, in respect of any demand prior to the bankruptcy, or which might be proved as a debt under the bankruptcy. Such creditor cannot prove without relinquishing his action, and the proving or claiming a debt under an adjudication by any creditor, shall be deemed an election by such creditor to take the benefit of the adjudication with respect to the debt so proved or claimed. There are provisions restoring the creditor in such a case to his former rights in case the petition for adjudication is dismissed.

Before proceeding to consider the means taken for the distribution of the estate collected, it seems convenient to take up and conclude the history of the Court's dealings with the bankrupt himself.

<small>Allowance to Bankrupts.</small>
I have pointed out the means placed at his disposal to contest his bankruptcy, if he thinks fit, and the statute makes provision for cases in which he can obtain the consent of a certain majority of his creditors to an order to annul the adjudication; but at present, considering him as a bankrupt, it is to be observed that until he shall have passed his last examination, or until it shall have been adjourned *sine die*, a majority in value of the creditors may grant him such allowance, from time to time, as may be necessary for the support of himself and his family; and he may also, after obtaining his certificate, receive a certain percentage out of, and calculated on, the produce of his realized estate, according to the 195th section of the Act of 1849. And in case of a joint adjudication of the joint estate and separate estate, if any partner have produced a sufficient dividend, he shall receive his allowance, although the other or others may not be so entitled. The policy of these provisions evidently is to encourage traders to come in time to the Court, and to reward them for securing some considerable estate for their creditors, by giving them a proportionate bonus out of their assets, so that they may start afresh in trade.

<small>Sitting for discharge of Bankrupt.</small>
Forthwith, after the meeting for the choice of an assignee by the creditors, the Court shall appoint a sitting not later than sixty days from the date of that meeting, for the bankrupt to pass his last examination and apply for his discharge.

The assignees, and any creditor who has proved, may be heard against the discharge.

If no order of discharge be made at such meeting the Court shall appoint a sitting for the purpose of considering the question of granting the bankrupt such order, of which sitting fourteen days' notice is to be given by newspaper advertisement.

In granting Orders of Discharge the following Rules must be observed.

<small>Order of discharge.</small>
In China and Japan, all orders as to the discharge of a bankrupt must be subject to appeal to the Supreme Court; and with regard to the provisions as to time, the Act of 1849, section 12 supplies a rule quite as applicable and proper here as in England.

Without a free right of appeal to a professional Court, the exercise of such a power would appear to be likely to be productive of much mischief; but it is right to say, that although the Consuls—in the great trading ports of the Levant at least—have been constantly called on to exercise, and have unquestionably exercised, a customary jurisdiction in Bankruptcy, the tendency has, so far as I can learn, invariably been to avoid extreme measures. And although this may have proceeded in part from a reasonable doubt as to the nature and extent of their power, it would be unfair not to attribute it in great part to a spirit of moderation and caution which, in the administration of the law, may be fairly said to be national, and which is certainly pleasing to observe, and creditable.

There can be no doubt, however, that absolute practical impunity for bankruptcies tainted with fraud is only too common; and on a

definite and settled jurisdiction, it will become the business of those who are entrusted with it in the first instance, to proceed with firmness in cases where the circumstances call for stricter measures; the right of appeal in all cases being freely allowed, and advice being applied for in cases of doubt or difficulty.

The effect of the discharge is to release the order of bankrupt from all debts due by him when he became bankrupt, and from all claims and demands made proveable under the bankruptcy, but it does not discharge any person who was a partner with him at the time of his bankruptcy, or was then jointly bound, or had made any joint contract with the bankrupt. *Effect of discharge.*

And if a bankrupt after his discharge is arrested, or has any action brought against him for any debt, claim, or demand proveable under his bankruptcy, he shall be discharged on appearing to the action, and may plead in general that the cause of action accrued before he became bankrupt, and give a certificate of the Act and the special matter in evidence. And the discharge is sufficient evidence of the bankruptcy, petition, and other proceedings precedent to it, and a bankrupt taken in execution on a judgment, previous to his discharge, may be discharged on production thereof. And, moreover, contracts or securities made or given by a bankrupt, or on his behalf, to a creditor, or in trust for him, to secure payment of money due by the bankrupt, as a consideration, or with intent to persuade such creditor to forbear opposition, or to consent to allowance of certificate, are void. *When may plead discharge.* *What contracts void.*

Any creditor obtaining money, goods, or security as an inducement for forbearing to oppose, or for consenting to the certificate, forfeits treble the value so obtained; and the bankrupt, after his discharge, is not liable to pay any debt, or demand, from which the order discharges him, upon any contract or promise made after the filing of the petition for adjudication.

But if the bankrupt is not discharged, he remains subject to all debts owing by him, and to all claims and demands, proved or proveable, under his bankruptcy, just as if he never had become bankrupt.

To complete the history of the Court's dealings with the bankrupt, it might seem necessary that some account should be given of the provisions for bringing to trial and punishment a bankrupt charged with not surrendering, concealing property, destroying or falsifying books, obtaining goods within three months of the petition for adjudication, under false colour of ordinary dealing, with intent to defraud the owner thereof, and the like offences; but I have already pointed out the propriety of applying in all such cases to the Supreme Court for direction, before taking any step in a matter of such delicacy. *Criminal sections of Bankrupt Act.*

It now only remains to conclude the account of the steps taken for ascertaining the exact amount of the estate available for distribution, and for distributing it accordingly, which are taken, of course, whatever may be the result of the proceedings as to the bankrupt himself. *Dividend.*

At the expiration of four months from the adjudication or earlier if need to, the creditors assignee submits to a meeting of the creditors and, of which ten days notice is to be given, a statement of the bankrupt's estate, and of receipts and payments on account of it. The official assignee attends and examines the statement and any creditor who has proved may do so likewise and the meeting may if it please vote a dividend after making reasonable provision for future contingencies. The meeting may also determine whether any and what allowance shall be made to the bankrupt. Similar dividend meetings are to be held at successive periods of four months until the whole estate has been exhausted.

Every dividend meeting is a meeting at which a creditor may prove a debt, but if the debt is proved at a second or subsequent dividend meeting, it is not in the power of the creditor to disturb former dividends.

Consuls, however, in considering claims to prove, will naturally, when refusing to admit them, exercise caution in parting with the money to the other creditors, until the result of an appeal to the Supreme Court is known.

In cases where an appeal in such a matter is merely made to delay the rights of others, the Court above would probably award exemplary costs.

Besides the ordinary provisions for the regular course of a bankruptcy, the Act of 1861, (sections 192 to 200 inclusive,) contains enactments regulating the manner in which a trader may, if unable to meet his engagements, make, if he can, an arrangement with a certain proportion of his creditors which shall bind the whole, or those at least who receive proper notices, either before or after bankruptcy.

The proceedings ought to be kept regularly, and the proofs of debts should be put in writing, and a note of their admission or rejection should be placed on them. The proceedings in a bankruptcy ought to be in such a form that the file may contain an exact history of it from its commencement to its conclusion; the first step being the petition for adjudication, and every subsequent step being recorded.

In England, all the proceedings, which are always reduced to writing, are placed on paper of a defined and uniform size; and, where possible, this should be done for convenience of reference. The Consul's notes of evidence are, no doubt, taken in his own book, but in this, as in other instances, a copy of them should accompany the proceedings in every case of appeal.

Under the Order in Council the several Provincial Courts are auxiliary to each other in Bankruptcy for the proof of debts and other matters, but the Supreme Court at Shanghai should be considered, as far as circumstances will admit, as standing in the place of the Central Court of Bankruptcy, while it also exercises the appeal jurisdiction which in England is vested in the Lord Chancellor and the Lords Justices of Appeal.

Probate.

I do not think it necessary to enlarge on the subject of Probate and Administration, as the duties of a Consul are fully defined in the Order in Council and the Rules, and as in every case of doubt or difficulty, the Consul is expressly required to refer to the Supreme Court for directions.

But I would specially direct attention to the provision of the Order in Council which renders any person other than the Consul liable to a heavy penalty who, without authority, takes possession of, and in any manner administers any part of the personal property of a deceased person. The principle involved in this provision is one which should be strictly enforced, and all unauthorised intermeddling with the property of deceased persons should be in every way discouraged and repressed. *Penalty on unauthorized persons dealing with an Estate.*

For the purpose of enabling the officers to charge the proper fees, all petitions seeking to recover money either as a debt or as damages should contain a distinct statement in words and figures of the total amount sought to be recovered, and no decree should be made for the recovery of a greater sum than that claimed in the petition, except for interest, where it is allowed by law, and the costs of the suit itself. *Fees.*

In cases where the result of the suit, or the decree of the Court, may enable a petitioner to recover any sum of money not directly and specifically sought, as in suits for dissolution of partnership and taking accounts, the Court should make special orders during the progress of the suit for ensuring the payment of the fees which would have become payable had the amount of money which the plaintiff may become entitled to recover, been asked for by the petition.

A few words relative to the provisions of the Order in Council and Rules respecting criminal cases will suffice, as the provisions themselves are very full and explicit. *Criminal Jurisdiction.*

The distinction between cases to be disposed of summarily, and those that are to be tried on indictment and with assessors, should be strictly observed, and the Consul should remember that as to cases of the latter class, he has no power to dispose of them summarily even where the accused openly admits his guilt. All such cases must go to trial in the regular form.

On a charge being made, to whichever class the case belongs, the Consul should not in the first instance issue a warrant for the apprehension of the accused, but should only issue a summons, except where from the nature of the offence, the character of the person charged, the probability of his absconding or other similar reason there is good ground to suspect that the ends of justice will be defeated by giving him notice. A man ought not without urgent necessity incur the loss of liberty until he has had a fair opportunity of answering the charge against him. *When warrant of arrest to issue.*

The Consul should in all cases avoid imposing unnecessary restraint upon the person charged, particularly where, having been served with a summons, he has appeared thereto at the proper time. When he is committed for safe custody during an adjournment, the adjournment should be for the shortest time consistent with the objects of the adjournment.

It is the duty of the person charging in every case, except where the person charged pleads guilty, to substantiate his charge; and if he be himself a witness, he will not be allowed to address the Court, except upon oath.

In cases which are to be tried on indictment, the preliminary examination cannot be proceeded with in the absence of the accused. *Examination should be in presence of accused.*

The charge should be first read over to the accused, but he is not to be called upon to plead. The case is to be substantiated against him in the first instance. The same rules of evidence are to be acted upon as if the case were being finally heard and determined.

Where in a case which is not to be determined summarily, the evidence for the prosecution on the preliminary examination fails to make out a *primâ facie* case, and the accused is discharged, he may be again apprehended on the same charge if additional facts against him should transpire.

If upon the apprehension of the accused any of his property be taken from him for safe custody, the Consul may, at his discretion, order it, or any part of it, to be restored or applied for the purpose of his defence.

If the accused be detained in custody to await his trial, he should be allowed to communicate with his friends and advisers under such regulations as the Consul may think proper.

When two or more parties are accused. When two (or more) parties are accused of the same offence committed at the same place and time and in concert the one with the other, the law requires that (when both are under arrest, or can be captured within a reasonable time) they shall be placed *together* in the dock and tried *together*. The accused parties cannot be permitted, or rather cannot be called upon, to give evidence for the other's defence. Criminality might never be established if the prisoners were allowed reciprocally to give exculpatory evidence in behalf of each other. A magistrate cannot refuse however to listen to anything an accused party may say either of himself or of any one else, if pertinent to the matter in hand; and any such statement, *as against the party making it*, is to a certain extent evidence, but it is not evidence, in the strict legal sense of the term in favour of an accomplice, although it is entitled to a certain amount of consideration more especially when it is confirmed by other evidence. As I have elsewhere observed, it is far better that Consuls, who are generally unprofessional men, should learn to the admission of all evidence or rather testimony which tends to throw a light on the subject under their consideration than to its exclusion. They must be careful however in the estimation of its value, to consider the circumstances under which it is given—the inducement of the party offering it to speak the truth—or to speak falsely.

King's Evidence. What is called "king's evidence" can only be given by one of the accused, after he has *confessed the extent of his own participation* in the crime, and where the charge could not be brought home to the other or others without his *damnatory* evidence; and in such cases (which occur very rarely) the accomplice thus admitted as king's evidence himself *escapes punishment*.

Illness, &c. of witnesses. In the case of a witness not attending on a summons in summary proceedings, a warrant to compel his attendance should not be issued if it appears that his failure to attend was caused by illness, attendance elsewhere in discharge of a public duty, or other urgent cause, care being taken however that the ends of justice are not defeated by the delay.

Accused party entitled to summonses for witnesses. Any person committed for trial is entitled on application at any time between his commitment and his trial to obtain on application,

either by himself or his legal advisers, summonses for any witnesses whose attendance he desires to secure at his trial, if such witnesses are British subjects. And in those cases where the prisoner desires the attendance of witnesses who are not British subjects, he may obtain on application a note to the respective Consulates of those witnesses asking for an order on them to attend.

I may here perhaps mention that although the punishment on a conviction for an injury to the person is usually considered a sufficient penalty—yet the party injured is not debarred from pursuing his civil remedy for compensation for the losses—in other words—the damages sustained by him in consequence and as a result of the injury inflicted. Damages in cases of assault.

The Criminal process is at the suit of the Crown, and although the real Prosecutor is the party injured, still it is the public that are outraged by the commission of the act and it is the Representative and Guardian of the public that seeks the infliction of the punishment. It is true that under the 74 Rule of the Rules of Procedure—the Court may on a conviction order that the accused pay all the expenses incident to the trial, and I have more than once, when medical attendance on the party injured had been absolutely necessary to enable him to appear and give his evidence, considered such Medical Expenses as incident to the trial and ordered their payment by the party convicted. In the same way I have also directed that the Expenses of the Prosecutor's Witnesses should be defrayed by the party convicted.

The Civil remedy is by an Action of Trespass as it is technically called—Trespass meaning a wrong—in which the injured party sets forth the assault—the injuries received—enumerates the damage occasioned him—the Expenses he may have been put to—and finally prays that the Party committing the assault may be condemned to pay him a sum sufficient to cover them in the shape of damages. Civil remedy.

The Defendant may plead to such an Action—either that he did not commit the assault or that he was justified in committing it—alleging some reason—such as being first assaulted by the Plaintiff—self defence—and a variety of other grounds. If he fails in establishing any such defences—damages may be given for the actual reasonable expenses incurred and the losses sustained, provided they are real actual losses and not problematical only—and if the injury is one that is lasting and certain to result in an inability, more or less great, to work at the injured party's pursuit or trade whatever it may be, I see no objection to compensation being given for such a wrong in the sense of damages. But it must be recollected that except under Lord Campbell's Act 9 and 10 Vict. Ch. 93, no civil action for damages can be maintained by the family or Legal representatives of a man who has died from the result of injuries received. His remedy dies with him. *See* Stephen's Blackstone 4 Vol. P. 91.

A Defendant may also under a Plea denying the assault, give in evidence extenuating circumstances, not amounting to a justification, in order to reduce the damages, but if the evidence is of a nature calculated to justify the assault, he must specially plead—in other words in his answer, he must state the circumstances upon which he relies as justifying the assault or other trespass which he admits to have committed, and the Judge ought then to take into consideration —in the *first* case whether the circumstances brought forward in *extenuation* are of a character to justify him in reducing the damages, which in the absence of them he would have felt it just and right to award—and in the *second* case whether the justification pleaded and the facts adduced in evidence in support of this defence really afford an excuse for the wrong done—if it does, no damages ought to be given.

Other Judicial duties of Consuls.

I have now only, in conclusion, to address you very shortly with reference to another branch of your judicial duties; I allude to that in which you are called upon by British subjects to support their claims either upon Chinese or Japanese subjects or upon Provincial Governments, and also to that in which you are asked by the local authorities to order a British subject to do or forbear to do a particular act.

Advancing claims of British subjects.

With regard to advancing the claims of British subjects, the best course is always to compel the party applying for your assistance to lay the particulars of his claim before you, with a précis of such evidence as he intends to bring forward in support of it, in order that you may make up your mind as to its justice and as to the sufficiency of the evidence.

To urge or support an unjust claim is beneath the dignity of any British agent, and it is inexpedient to put any claim forward that cannot be supported by a fair amount of reasonable evidence. I do not go the length of saying that there are not a class of claims which appeal more to a sense of justice and equity, for their consideration and admission, than to any legal amount of technical proof, nor do I mean to say that Consuls should not present and urge such claims upon the local authorities; but it will be well to examine carefully each case, and only to advance such as fall clearly within the category to which I have alluded.

Colourable British claims.

And this appears to me to be a convenient place to warn Consuls against being entrapped into advancing claims which are only colourably British claims, but in which, in reality, no British subject has an interest, except in respect of the price which may be payable to him for the use of his name and the protection of his Consulate. Foreigners sometimes, and Native born subjects of the Emperor of China or Chief Authority of Japan not unfrequently, assign over to British subjects claims which they have upon the local authorities, or upon individuals that may be subject to the local authorities, for the express purpose of enlisting the power and influence of British Consuls to obtain a settlement. Such assignments, however, are clearly illegal as against the third person, and under no circumstances should Consuls act upon them. Of course I do not speak of assignments by way of endorsement of negotiable instruments; such are permitted by the usages of trade, and are not assignments of claims in the sense in which I have used the word.

As a general rule, therefore, the claimant should first submit his case to the Consul whose aid he seeks, with a statement of the evidence or proof which he has to support it, and the Consul should then carefully consider it, and if, in his judgment, more evidence is required, he should take care that the plaintiff procures it, so that

he may advance it in the way which he, the Consul, thinks most calculated to ensure success, and, at the same time, with all necessary completeness. Moderation in demands, and firmness in their prosecution, will, at any rate, create confidence, even when, in particular cases, it is found impossible to obtain all that is asked.

When Interpreters are instructed to present and support the claim before the local authorities, they should always be furnished with written instructions, and required to make written reports. This course of practice is advisable, because it enables the Consul, at any subsequent period, as well as during the course of the inquiry, to test the manner in which his orders have been obeyed. *Instructions to Interpreters.*

In those cases where the local authorities request the assistance of the Consul, such request (which should always be made in writing) should also, when the circumstances of the case admit of it, and justice is not likely to be defeated by the delay, be communicated in writing to the parties affected by it; and this written request should descend to such particulars as to enable the Consul to form an opinion as to the course he ought to pursue. It is always advisable, in the first instance, to cite the person complained against before you, in order that you may communicate the nature of the request, and hear what he has to say; in short, to get from him an explanation, and according to that explanation being satisfactory or the reverse, should the course taken be regulated.

If it is perfectly satisfactory, and is supported by evidence which establishes its truth, a written statement, in which this explanation should be shortly condensed, should be sent to the local authority, with an offer to substantiate it when required. If, however, the explanation is unsatisfactory, or full of suspicion, or there are circumstances which induce a strong belief that the British subject is wrong, then in a flagrant case I should advise prompt acquiescence in the request made; but, if the wrong be not flagrant, the British subject should be sent before the competent Court to take his trial.

In civil cases, and indeed in all cases, it is expedient to insist upon a proper trial, conducted according to form, and an exercise of extraordinary judicial power should never be willingly resorted to by the Consul, or tolerated by him on the part of the local authority. At the same time there are cases where its exercise, from motives of public policy, becomes necessary, and in some it may be even tolerated when exercised by the local authorities: but the treatment of such cases must be left to individual discretion, and Consuls will seldom err if they bear in mind that their chief object should be so to regulate their own proceedings as to furnish a bright example of order, method, and perfect impartiality, towards the parties and to the local authorities, and they should always so act as to be capable at any moment to give due and sufficient reasons for the course pursued.

In cases where the local authorities are manifestly acting in a partial and improper manner, the Consul should place before them, in writing, a précis of the case, pointing out where and how they are acting contrary to law and to justice; and having done this, and having fully, and to the best of his ability explained to them, *vivâ voce*, the reasons why he objects to the course pursued, he should then protest, and forward his protest, with the précis of the case, to the Supreme Court, who will either give him instructions how to proceed, or prefer the case to Her Majesty's Minister for his interposition in the proper Quarter.

In criminal charges, either against British subjects or against subjects of the Emperor of China or the Chief Authority of Japan at the instance of British subjects, great regularity and order should be observed and insisted upon.

No man should be arrested and deprived of his liberty, except upon grave suspicion of having done that for which he ought to suffer punishment.

The responsibility of proving the truth of the accusation should rest on the accuser, and he should be compelled to substantiate his charge within as short a time as possible; and if delay is absolutely necessary to enable him to collect his evidence, such delay should not, except in extreme cases, be permitted to prejudice the position of the accused. In the greatest number of cases, bail for the appearance of the accused, when called upon to take his trial, should be accepted. Of course, exceptions must be made in those cases where the suspicion of guilt is so strong as to raise a very fair presumption that the accused will sacrifice his bail or guarantee, rather than appear and take his trial; but such cases will be few.

The greatest care must at all times be taken that the accused has every means afforded him before trial, by communication with his friends, or legal adviser, if he has one, of rebutting the evidence against him, and establishing his innocence; and no opportunity should be lost of inculcating upon the local authorities that the object of criminal law and criminal procedure is not so much to prove that an accused person is guilty of the offence with which he is charged, as to enable the accuser to prove the guilt which he imputes, and, at the same time, afford to the accused every fair means of defending himself.

To this end, the Consul should take care that the accuser is obliged to state on oath or in some form binding on his conscience according to the Laws of his Country, all the facts upon which he relies to establish the truth of his accusation. His witnesses should be obliged to do the same. Both he and they should not be allowed to adduce hearsay evidence, or that which they heard other persons say, but such testimony should at once be rejected, and the persons alluded to, be themselves produced.

It is expedient, likewise, to allow the prisoner a full opportunity of cross-examining all the persons giving evidence, and, having done so, he should be permitted to make any statement he likes, and call what witnesses he choses in support of his explanation.

Every care should be taken to expose any animus with which the accuser or witnesses may be inspired.

In short, while on the one hand, it is the Consul's business to see that justice is done and crime punished, it is, on the other hand, his duty to take care that it is properly proved, and that the accused has every reasonable chance afforded him. His assent to a fair judgment, arrived at after due investigation of the facts, should never be withheld; while at the same time, both before trial and at the

trial, he should, at least, insist upon throwing the whole onus of proof on the accuser, and prevent conclusions being adopted founded rather upon moral convictions than upon clear and distinct evidence.

In many police cases, he will have to assist in deciding, upon the truth, or the balance of truth, on conflicting statements. He must do so on mature deliberation, giving the accused the benefit of all reasonable doubt, and, at the same time, duly considering probabilities and all other attendant circumstances which may go towards establishing a conclusion, based on proved facts, either of guilt or innocence.

With reference to protesting against any deviation from right and justice on the part of the local authorities, he will pursue the same course as I have already pointed out in civil cases.

NOTIFICATION.

WHEREAS it has been brought to my knowledge that British subjects of Chinese descent having all the appearance of Chinese and speaking like natives, established themselves in the interior of the country and permanently take up their residence there, acquiring all the privileges of Chinese subjects in violation of Treaty provisions governing the status and acts of British subjects in the Chinese dominions, it is hereby publicly notified, that any one so offending is liable to be taken by the Chinese authorities to the nearest Consular Port to be handed over to the British Consul for punishment, in the same way as any other class of British subject would be punished for a similar violation of Treaty.

RUTHERFORD ALCOCK,
H. M.'s Envoy Extraordinary, Minister Plenipotentiary and Chief Superintendent of Trade in China.

Peking, November 28th, 1866.

NOTIFICATION.

By direction of Sir RUTHERFORD ALCOCK, K. C. B., Her Britannic Majesty's Envoy Extraordinary, Minister Plenipotentiary, and Chief Superintendent of British Trade in China.—Three Regulations are published below for the Registration of Mortgages, the Registration of Bills of Sale, and the Registration of Companies in China. The Regulations for the Registration of Mortgages and Bills of Sale have been approved by Her Majesty's Government. The Regulation affecting Registration of Companies, will equally with the others take effect until the farther pleasure of Her Majesty's Government be made known.

THOMAS FRANCIS WADE,
Secy. of Legation.

Peking, 11th July, 1866.

I. REGULATION.

("China and Japan Order in Council, 1865," Sec. VII., Clause 85.)

All mortgage of lands and houses, legal or equitable, must be registered at the Consulate of the district in which the property is situated, within fourteen days of the date of the execution of the deed.

If such mortgage is made in any Consular district in China other than that in which the property is situated, then the same must be registered within such Consular district within fourteen days of the execution of the deed, and within two months of such execution in the Consulate of the district wherein the property is situated.

If such deed is executed in Hongkong then the same must be registered within such Consular district as aforesaid within two months of such execution; and if the deed be executed elsewhere than in China, Japan, or Hongkong, then the same must be registered at the Consulate of the district within which the property is situated, within six months of such execution; otherwise such Mortgage Deed will not be allowed precedence over judgment or simple contract debts, contracted before the execution of such deed.

On every registration a fee of five dollars will be payable, and on every inspection of books of registry, a fee of one shilling.

II. REGULATION.

("China and Japan Order in Council, 1865," Sec. VII., Clause 85.)

For preventing frauds on creditors, notice is hereby given that all Bills of Sale, and every Schedule or Inventory annexed thereto or referred to therein must within 21 days after the making thereof be filed in the Supreme Court or in the Consular Court of the District in which the property mentioned in such Bill of Sale is situated, together with an affidavit of the time when the same was made, and a description of the residence and occupation of the person making it, and of every attesting witness; and any defeazance, condition, or declaration of trust, to which such Bill of Sale is subject, must be written in the body of it, or annexed thereto.

The fee payable on the filing of such Bill of Sale shall be one dollar, and for the affidavit also one dollar.

III. REGULATION.

Affecting Co-Partnerships, the members of which are unknown, or which carry on trade by Agents.

Co-partnerships all of whose members are not known.

Whereas in some cases business is or may be carried on in Shanghai and elsewhere in China by persons in co-partnership, or by one individual or more assuming the style of a co-partnership, or acting as agent or agents of a co-partnership, and in some of those cases the members of such co-partnership, or some of them, are not only absent from the place where such co-partnership business is carried on, but their names are or may be unknown; Be it therefore enacted

and ordained. That (in order to prevent any failure of justice in such cases,) every such co-partnership, and the several members thereof, or the persons or person having carried, or carrying on business under the style of any such co-partnership, may be sued in any action at law in the name or names of any one or more of the members of such co-partnership on behalf of all the members comprising the same, or in the name or names of any such agent or agents for and on behalf of such co-partnership, so as that, in all cases wherein but for this regulation it would have been necessary to mention the names of all the members comprising such co-partnership, it shall be sufficient to mention the name or names of such one or more member or members only, or of such agent or agents on behalf of such co-partnership.

<small>Such co-partnerships may be sued in the name of any one member or agent.</small>

And be it ordered. That every judgment obtained or made in any such action as last aforesaid, shall have the same effect and operation upon the person and property both real and personal of such co-partnership, and of the several members thereof, whether such property be joint or separate, as if every member of such co-partnership had been actually and in fact a defendant in the action, and every such judgment or order may be enforced against all such property as in ordinary cases of the like nature.

<small>Judgment against such defendant to operate against the co-partnership.</small>

Provided always and be it ordered. That in every summons and other writ issued, and declaration or other pleading filed, on behalf of the Plaintiff in any action brought under the provisions of the two preceeding sections, the style of firm of the co-partnership shall be specified, and it shall distinctly appear, that the Defendant or Defendants sued is or are so sued for and on behalf of such Co-partnership: and provided also, that no Agent sued on behalf of any such Co-partnership shall by reason only of his being so sued, be incompetent as a Witness in the action on behalf either of the Plaintiff or the Co-partnership, or be liable in person or property to any judgment obtained in such action.

<small>Proviso.</small>

<small>Agent not to be incompetent as witness.</small>

And (for supplying a more full and effectual remedy in this behalf) in all cases in which there are Joint Contractors, one or more of whom shall be absent from the place wherein the contract was made, or where the cause of action arising out the contract arose—Be it ordered, That no plea in abatement shall hereafter be received on behalf of any Defendant in any action in respect of the non-joinder therein of any person alleged to have been a joint contractor with such defendant, unless it be expressly alleged in such plea, that the person not joined, is then resident at some place within the Consular district wherein the trade of the Co-partnership is carried on, or where the cause of action arose.

<small>Plea in abatement.</small>

NOTIFICATION.

WHEREAS it has been brought to my notice that divers Persons, British Subjects, frequent the Foreign Settlements at the Treaty Ports, and there remain, having no ostensible means of livelihood or settled occupation, and that it is to be feared that such Persons live by the Commission of Crime, by robbery or plunder; and whereas it is desirable and of urgent necessity, not only for the maintenance of friendly relations with the Authorities of China and the Subjects of His Imperial Majesty, but also for the maintenance of peace, order and good government of British Subjects residing in or resorting to China, that a stop should be put to such lawless proceedings: Therefore by the authority and power vested in me by the 85th Section of the China and Japan Order in Council 1865, I do declare and order that it shall be lawful for and the duty of Her Majesty's Judicial Officers from time to time, and when it shall appear necessary, to summon before them and enforce the attendance of all persons who, it may be reported to them, have no ostensible means of livelihood, and then and there require of such persons to state and where expedient to produce evidence of the means they possess of subsistence; and should it appear that such persons possess no ostensible means of livelihood, then it shall be lawful for such Judicial Officers to order that such persons shall inform the Court of their place of residence, and shall also report themselves to such persons as the Judicial Officers aforesaid shall direct, at such times and with such formalities as shall be then directed: and any neglect in obeying any Order thus given shall render the person guilty of the disobedience liable to imprisonment for a term not exceeding ten days or deportation from China, and to be detained in custody until a fit time and opportunity for his deportation arrives.

And in consideration of the urgent necessity for this Regulation, I further order that it shall have effect unless and until it is disapproved by Her Most Gracious Majesty and notification of such disapproval is received and published by me in China.

Given under my hand and Seal this 14th day of January, 1867.

L. S.

(Signed)   RUTHERFORD ALCOCK,
H. M.'s Envoy Extraordinary and Minister Plenipotentiary and Chief Superintendent of Trade in China.

CIRCULAR NOTIFICATION.

SOME misunderstanding appears to prevail as to the course to be pursued by Her Majesty's Consular Officers with regard to the Estates of Intestates.

Consular Courts have within their several districts power to grant Probate of Wills and also Administration where there is no contention respecting the right to the grant—(see Section 57 of the China and Japan Order in Council, 1865). Where no person having the right to claim Administration of the Estate of a deceased British

Subject, appears to demand a grant of it, it is the duty of the Consul to take possession of the Estate for safe custody as, until Administration is granted, the personal property of an Intestate vests in the Judge of the Supreme Court (see Section 59 of the Order in Council).

A Consul, therefore, should ascertain of what property the deceased died possessed, where it is situated, its amount, and every particular connected with it. He should then—having when necessary taken possession of it, or, when the actual taking possession is uncalled for, after taking an Inventory of it and a Receipt from the Person in whose custody it is left—immediately communicate all the information he has collected, to the Judge of the Supreme Court and await his directions.

In most cases, and especially where the value of the property as is most generally the case, is trifling, the Judge will desire the Consul to sell the property, reserving such personal trinkets, &c. &c., as relatives are generally desirous of having sent to them, and with the proceeds pay any trifling and immediate debts which may be owing, such as Funeral Expenses, Servant's Wages, Arrears of Rent, Doctor's Bills, &c. &c., and remit the balance with an Account of Receipts and Payments to the Supreme Court.

When however the Estate is considerable, the Judge will generally and under certain circumstances appoint an Official Administrator to administer the Estate.

Until however the instructions of the Judge of the Supreme Court are received, Consuls have no authority to interfere with an Intestate Estate (except so far as ensuring its safe custody) in respect of which no one claims or is in a position to claim.

Administration and all so called Official Administration by Consuls except under the express Authority of Judge, is contrary to the Order in Council.

With reference to the Estates in respect of which Administration has been granted by a Provincial Court, all that a Consul has to do is to fill up Form No. 30 and transmit the same every half year to the Supreme Court.

H. B. M's. SUPREME COURT,
  SHANGHAI;
 23rd January, 1867.

INDEX.

INDEX OF CONTENTS.

A

	Page:
ACCOUNTS, question of, may be referred........................	33
ACCUSED, see CRIMINAL JURISDICTION.	
ACT, MERCHANT SHIPPING, see MERCHANT SHIPPING ACT.	
—— OF BANKRUPTCY, see BANKRUPTCY ACT.	
ADJOURNMENTS in the hearing of cases to be avoided ...	31
ADMINISTRATION, LETTERS OF, see PROBATE.	
ADMIRALTY jurisdiction, nature of...............................	14
Supreme Court alone is a Court of	9, 14
Consuls, however, should know the functions of the Supreme Court in the matter	14
AFFIDAVITS in motion to shew cause, to be filed at the Consulate	34
, rules as to (Rules of Procedure 230-42) 34, 35	
AGENTS AND PARTNERSHIPS, Rule recently framed for suits against...	35
Agent or Partner must be British subject	36
or Principals, which? great care necessary	29
AGREEMENT TO REFER questions of Fact or Law 26, 34	
AMENDMENTS TO PETITION AND ANSWER are to be freely allowed	54
expenses to be borne by the party amending	ib.
ANSWER TO PETITION may be amended by Consul, if necessary...	30
on oath	54
, procedure on	30, 52
should be short and relevant............................	43
when no answer is put in, presumptions and procedure in different cases	50
APPEAL TO SUPREME COURT	65
, course to follow in	21
fees to be previously paid	ib.
what payable to Consular Court	ib.
Supreme Court	ib.
from interlocutory orders	65
further evidence may be forwarded by Consul	ib.
mere irregularity will not suffice to disturb the original finding	61
on a special point	31
parties not required to attend	65

	Page.
[APPEAL TO SUPREME COURT]	
will be decided on the evidence given in the Court below	65
—— come on in rotation	ib.
—— lie on all Orders (not being *ex parte*) on a motion	34
APPLICATION TO SUITS, SPECIAL	43
, great danger of	44
how they arise	ib.
, several classes of	ib.
ARBITRATION should be encouraged	9, 40
ARREST OF THE PERSON	33
in cases of debt, under what circumstances permitted	ib.
in criminal cases, when to be resorted to	95
ASSAULT, DAMAGES FOR	97
civil remedy by action of " trespass "	ib.
defendant may deny the charge or plead extenuating circumstances	ib.
no civil action can be taken by the family, &c., of a man who dies from the injuries received	ib.
the party convicted may be ordered to pay all the expenses, medical, &c.	ib.
ASSESSORS, attendance cannot be compelled	5
, dissent of, from conviction	17
refusal to attend to be noted	5
ASSIGNEE, CREDITORS', see BANKRUPTCY.	
OFFICIAL, see BANKRUPTCY.	

B

BAIL, ORDERS TO HOLD TO	
Consul in all cases to exercise his discretion	46
may be the subject of a special application	44
, more care required in, when foreigners are the applicants	46
, what condition requisite before granting	44
claim for unliquidated damages not sufficient	45
"out of jurisdiction" how to be understood	ib.
BANKRUPT	
, allowance to	92
, criminal proceedings against	81, 93
, debts of, what are paid in full, or in larger proportion	86
apprentice p. 87, clerk 86, rent 87, workman ib.	
, debts of, payable on a contingency	88
, proof of	87
, appeal from	92
may be opposed by creditors' assignee	87
what proveable	ib.
, discharge, effect of	93
, order of	92
is subject to appeal to Supreme Court	ib.

	Page.
[BANKRUPT]	
discharge, sitting for	92
estates, Registry-book of, must be kept	30
estate to be secured	82
vests in assignees or the interest of the creditors	84
, fraudulent, to be punished	10
, goods in the order and disposition of, law as to	85
in formâ pauperis	11
letters may be intercepted by Court	84
must pay the fees and expenses incident to his bankruptcy	11
mutual debts	89
, parties suspected of collusion with, may be summoned by Court	84
partner separately adjudicated	90
search-warrants may be granted by Court	84
surrender of	83
wife may be examined by the Court	84
BANKRUPTCY, a Consular Court has jurisdiction in	9, 78
,. acts of, two classes of	79
, adjudication of	80
, how obtained by a creditor	79
joint creditors	80
the debtor himself	ib.
must be advertised in the most public way	ib.
proceedings after	81
proceedings for annulling after the allow-[ed term has elapsed	83
—— before the allowed term has elapsed	ib.
service of	ib.
creditors, first meeting of	ib.
second meeting of	84
creditors' (or trade) assignee	82
can oppose proof of debts	87
have to bring actions and defend same	85
may be removed by Court	ib.
recover bankrupt's property	86
when chosen	85
dividend	93
fees and expenses incident to, must be paid by the Bankrupt	11
mortgagees	89
of an agent	ib.
official assignee, duties of	82
proceedings in, full account of, must be kept	94
sales by auction in	86
ACT, no fraudulent debtor should be allowed to escape under the	10, 79
proceedings must be taken within the time specified in the, and in accordance with the	11, 78

Page.
[BANKRUPTCY]
LAW, at present in a transitory and uncertain state ...10, 78
    object of 79
    what will be its general tenor when determined... 10
BARRING PROCEEDINGS, ... 66
    under what circumstances this power will be exercised ib.
BREACHES OF CONTRACT, PENALTY FOR, see
    DAMAGES.
OF THE PEACE, continuous offences may be construed
    as.. 19
    how provided against .... ib.
    —— punished .... ib.
    what security must be taken............................. ib.
BRITISH SUBJECTS, death of, proceedings in case of...... 15
    may submit cases between themselves and foreigners
    to the award of the foreigners' Consuls 21
, NATURALIZED, Chinese (or Japanese, see page 4)
    have no right beyond the particular colony or pos-
    session in which they are 3
    have the same disabilities as native-born subjects ... 4
    , what are to be considered as 3
    when jurisdiction can be exercised over them.......... ib.

C

CASES, Half-yearly Return of, to be sent to Supreme Court 8
    , Headings of Entry of, in Judge's Note-book 23
    should be brought on for hearing without delay...... 26
        taken in their turn 54
CAUSE, MOTIONS TO SHOW, see MOTIONS TO SHOW
    CAUSE.
CHINESE NATURALIZED BRITISH SUBJECTS, see
    BRITISH SUBJECTS, NATURALIZED.
SUBJECT as plaintiff or defendant against British Sub-
    ject, see LOCAL AUTHORITIES AND CONSUL.
CIRCULAR LETTER TO LEVANT CONSULS, Extract
    from ....39 et seq.
CIVIL CASES, essential nature of................................... 41
    for administration of property of deceased persons... ib.
    form the bulk of judicial suits .... ib.
    summary procedure on bills of exchange................ ib.
    under £100 are by summary procedure .... ib.
CLAIMS, divided into defective and bad 42
    force of this distinction .... ib.
    result of bad claims 43
        defective claims 42
COMMITTEE OF LAND RENTERS, see MUNICIPAL
    COUNCIL.
COMPELLING PROCEEDINGS in cases commenced 65
    Court to decide if delay is reasonable 66
COMPENSATION BY WAY OF DAMAGES, see DAMAGES.

	Page.
CONSANGUINITY, degrees of	16
CONSUL and Local Authorities, see LOCAL AUTHORITIES AND CONSULS.	
and Municipal Council of Port, relations between, see MUNICIPAL COUNCIL AND CONSUL.	
can act as Coroner	9
how to act in advancing claims of British subjects	98
—— when matters are referred to him for arbitration	8
—— proceed on a Warrant of Execution issued by Supreme Court	ib.
in what cases can charge percentage on Estates of Deceased Persons	29
may act as Registrar of his Court in Bankruptcy ...	11
—— elicit before trial, by *vivâ voce* interrogation, the question in dispute	26
—— issue a warrant for distress on behalf of landlord	36
Minute of Proceedings, see MINUTE OF PROCEEDINGS.	
must have sufficient evidence of the justice of a claim before he gives it his official aid	98
—— inspect the body of a foreigner in British employ who dies under suspicious circumstances ...	12
—— not advance claims that are put forward under the name only of British subjects	98
—— prepare Jury lists for the Supreme Court	5
, other judicial duties of, see LOCAL AUTHORITIES AND CONSUL.	
to send to Supreme Court Half-yearly Return of cases	8
CONSULAR AGENT, doubtful whether he may solemnise marriage	4
not included in Section 25 of Order	ib.
COURTS are Courts of Record	5
auxiliary to each other, in what sense, and to what extent	8, 40
can not hold jury trials	5
can only be held by Commissioned Consular Officers	4
, functions of	9
, jurisdiction of, nature of,	40
generally to decide for themselves	6
may reserve decision on a special point for the Supreme Court	31
special cases how provided for	6
what crimes punishable by	16
when to refer to Supreme Court	6
OFFICERS cannot enact Ordinances on their own responsibility	3, 38
especially necessary that they should have some knowledge of law	1
should know *where* to find the law on any subject...	2
, to hold a Court, must have a Commission from Her Majesty	4

[CONSULAR]
    ORDINANCES, what are not repealed 3
                        repealed .... ib.
CONTEMPT OF COURT 62
CONTRACT, PENALTY FOR BREACH OF, see DAMAGES.
CORONER, Consul can act as 9
    'S INQUEST, general outline of proceedings at a.......... 13
               what are fit cases for a......................... 11
    JURY, form of Oath for 12
               Summons for 13
      , verdict of .... ib.
COSTS, how much to be awarded 24, 69
    in Interlocutory Proceedings, rule as to ....ib. ib.
    to be fixed at time of delivering judgment ....ib. ib.
COUNCIL, MUNICIPAL, see MUNICIPAL COUNCIL.
COURT at Hongkong, when it has jurisdiction 19
    contempt of.. 62
    of Record, what is a 5
    , CONSULAR, see CONSULAR COURT.
    , SUPREME, see SUPREME COURT.
CREDITORS' ASSIGNEE, see BANKRUPTCY.
CRIMES, what are punishable by a Consular Court 16
CRIMINAL JURISDICTION 95
    accused is entitled to summonses for witnesses ...... ·96
    to be allowed communication with his friends
        and advisers .... ib.
    when several are implicated in the same case,
        to be tried together .... ib.
    distinction between summary cases and indictment
        cases to be observed 95
    examination must be in presence of accused .... ib.
    nature of king's (or queen's) evidence 96
    neither of the accused can give exculpatory evidence
        for the other .... ib.
    presence of witnesses, when not compellable by
        warrant .... ib.
    warrant of arrest to be issued only when absolutely
        necessary 95
CROSS-EXAMINATION OF WITNESSES 60
    permitted only on material points 62
CROSS-SUITS 67

D

DAMAGES 69
    as compensation 73
    , compound interest allowed on, only from express
        contract or custom.......................... 72
    , consequential 76
    , excessive, a ground of appeal............ 78

Page.
[DAMAGES]
, exemplary, ...77, 78
for breach of contract ... 73
non-delivery of goods ... 76
non-payment of money ... ib.
generally a sufficient remedy for non-performance of contract ... 69
in action of "detinue," ... 77
"tort" ... ib.
"trover" ... ib.
— cases of assault (see also ASSAULT, DAMAGES FOR) 97
, interest depending on, compound, when allowed... 72
Court to exercise discretion in awarding ib.
in the case of awards... 72
bills of exchange... 71
bonds ... 72
particular instances ... 71
when allowed ... 70
when compulsory ... 71
when not allowed ... ib.
"liquidated damages" and "penalty," distinction between ... 74
instance of ... ib.
real intention of the parties is the guide 75
instance ... ib.
, special ... 77
, uncertain ... 76
, unliquidated, meaning of the term ... 70
no interest chargeable on ... 71
when none are fixed ... 76
DEAD BODY OF A FOREIGNER in British employ, the Consul must, in suspicious cases, examine ... 12
DEATH OF A BRITISH SUBJECT, proceedings in case of 15
DEBTOR, JUDGMENT, see JUDGMENT DEBTOR.
DECEASED PERSONS, ESTATE OF, registry-book must be kept ... 29
, when Consul can charge percentage on ... ib.
DECISION on a special point may be referred to the Supreme Court ... 31
, speedy, required ... 26
DECREE, final, or interlocutory... 63
ON JUDGMENT, see JUDGMENT, Order on.
DEFENCES in confession and avoidance, definition of examples,... 53
DELAY in decision very prejudicial ... 26
in trial of cause, none to be accorded beyond that allowed by the Rules, ... 54
DEMURRER, what? ...30, 42
when defendant's objection as to Law is dismissed, he may object as to the Fact... 43

	Page.
DEPORTATION	19
DEPOSITIONS OF WITNESSES who may be leaving the locality, can be taken	56
DISSENT OF ASSESSORS to conviction	17
DISTRESS BY LANDLORD	36
affidavit in which the facts are stated, necessary	ib.
, mode of execution of warrant for	ib.
should be effected through Consul	ib.
tenant must be British subject	ib.
text-books referred to	37
DOCUMENTARY EVIDENCE, admission of	23
course to be taken when an objection is made to the	ib.
DUPLICATE OF PAPERS to be served in a suit, is required for the Courts	27

E

ENTRY OF PLAINT, example of	28
EQUITABLE DEFENCES	67
instances of	67, 8
EQUITY, what is	9, 67
, COURT OF, Consular Court is a	ib., ib.
its nature misunderstood	ib., ib.
ERRONEOUS action by Consuls, instance of	6
decision, instance of	73
notion of what Equity is	9
ESTATES OF BANKRUPTS, registry-book to be kept	30
DECEASED PERSONS, registry-book must be kept	29
when Consul can charge percentage on	ib.
, PARTNERSHIP, rule in cases of, where one partner dies	16
EVIDENCE,	
, collateral, to be generally rejected	58
distinction between what is sufficient and what is necessary	26
in the adversary's possession	59
—— possession of a person not under the Court's jurisdiction	60
legalized copies are evidence	59
may be given in a civil case by the parties themselves	23
on whom the burthen of proof lies	59
, "parol," when admissible	ib.
primary, what?	ib.
—— to be preferred to secondary	ib.
secondary, what?	ib.
want of procurable evidence not to be excused, and trial not to be postponed on that account	55
, DOCUMENTARY, admission of	23
proof as to handwriting	58
course to be taken when an objection is made	23
, HEARSAY, not admissible	58

	Page.
[EVIDENCE] OF EXPERTS, commonest form of	58
EXAMINATION OF WITNESSES	23
Cross-examination	60
only permitted on material points	62
EXECUTION AGAINST GOODS for non-compliance with Order of Judgment	32, 64
, caution to be exercised in the	6, 32, 64
Consul cannot refuse to grant	32
extreme and peculiar cases, procedure in	64
may issue from Supreme Court to Consular Court	8
OF JUDGMENTS	63
EXPENSES OF WITNESSES	24
EXPERTS, Evidence of	ib.
, Surveys, &c. of	ib.

F

FEE-BOOK must be kept	29
FEES FOR APPEAL to Supreme Court	
what payable to Consular Court	21
what payable, and when, to Supreme Court	ib.
FILING OF PAPERS, the, should be systematic	27
FINAL DECREE	63
FOREIGNER AS DEFENDANT, British Courts have no jurisdiction	20
Consular Officers may act as arbiters	21
AS PLAINTIFF, British Court have jurisdiction	20
IN BRITISH EMPLOY, if he dies under suspicious circumstances, Consul himself must view the body	12
not to be registered	20
ON THE MUSTER ROLL OF A BRITISH SHIP, when amenable and when not to British Consular jurisdiction	4
FORMS, value of, felt by many classes	25

G

GOODS, EXECUTION AGAINST, see EXECUTION AGAINST GOODS.

H

HEADINGS OF CASES in Judge's Note-book	23
HEARING, proceedings at, must be regular and orderly	57
proof how tendered	ib.
—— of all statements is necessary	ib.
Rules as to Lists generally to be observed	54

	Page.
[HEARING,]	
when and by whom postponements, &c., may be made	54
who should commence the pleadings? rule	56
HEARSAY EVIDENCE is not admissible	58
its most common form	ib.
HONGKONG, convicted offenders under what circumstances sent to	17
Court at, when it has jurisdiction	19

I

IMPRISONMENT	17
a more serious punishment in China than in England	ib.
under decrees in civil suits	64
INDEX TO RULES may be referred to with advantage	35
INJUNCTIONS	46
such must be "interim" orders	47
, EXPARTE	ib.
INQUEST, form of Inquisition at	14
, general outline of proceedings at	12, 13
must be held on the body	11
, remuneration to Medical officers serving on	12
, what a fit case for	11
, witness at, form of oath for	13
INQUISITION AT AN INQUEST, form of	14
INTEREST, claim of, arising out of a question of Damages, see DAMAGES.	
INTERLOCUTORY DECREE	63
PROCEEDINGS	33
, great care to be exercised in	33, 35
, object of	33
, rule as to costs in	34
should be noted in Judge's Minutes	55
INTERNATIONAL LAW, what is	2
works on, recommended	ib.
INTERPRETERS should have their instructions in writing	99
—— make written reports on the results of their negotiations with Authorities	ib.
INTRODUCTION	1
INVENTORY OF PROPERTY of deceased British subject, when to be taken	15
ISSUE, defined	25
, settlements of	30, 50
should be clearly developed in Petition and Answer	25
IN LAW AND ISSUE IN FACT, different means of determining	30

J

JAPANESE NATURALIZED BRITISH SUBJECTS, see under BRITISH SUBJECTS, NATURALIZED.

SUBJECT as plaintiff or defendant against British subject, see under LOCAL AUTHORITIES AND CONSULS.

	Page.
JUDGMENT completes the record	62
may be reserved, if necessary	31
need not be lengthy	62
to be given after hearing, if possible	31
DEBTOR, warrant may be issued against	32
EXECUTION OF	63
ORDER ON	31
, form of	ib.
, procedure on non-compliance with	32
SUMMONS, object of	ib.
, proceedings on	ib.
, when to issue	ib.

JURISDICTION, CRIMINAL, see CRIMINAL JURISDICTION.

OF CONSULAR COURT, nature of	40
JURY LIST, to be prepared by Consuls and sent to Supreme Court and Secretary of State	5
, TRIAL BY, limited to Supreme Court	ib.

K

KING'S (OR QUEEN'S) EVIDENCE, nature of	96

L

LANDLORD, DISTRESS BY, see DISTRESS BY LANDLORD.
LANDRENTERS, COMMITTEE OF, see MUNICIPAL COUNCIL.

LAW, Consul not expected to know *what* is the law on every subject, but to know *where* to find it in the commonest matters	2
, Consular Court is a Court of	9
, some knowledge of, especially necessary to Consular Officers	1
, text-book on, recommended	2
INTERNATIONAL, what is	ib.
works on, recommended	ib.
MUNICIPAL, OF ENGLAND, what is	ib.
OBJECTION IN,	
if established by Defendant, Plaintiff's case at once falls to the ground	30
if not established, the case proceeds to trial	ib.

	Page.
[LAW]	
OF BANKRUPTCY, at present in a transitory and uncertain state	10, 78
, no fraudulent debtor should be allowed to escape under the	10
what will be its general tenor when determined	ib.
LETTERS OF ADMINISTRATION, see PROBATE.	
LEVANT CONSULS, EXTRACT FROM CIRCULAR LETTER TO	39 et seq.
LOCAL AUTHORITIES AND CONSULS	98
action of Consul when assistance is asked by Authorities	99
Authorities are acting wrongly	ib.
application to Consul for assistance should be in writing, whether by British subjects or by Authorities	98, 99
cases between Chinese (or Japanese) and British subjects, great regularity to be observed in trial of all	100
accused should be allowed to cross-examine and call witnesses for his defence	ib.
—— to have communication with his friends and advisers	ib.
accuser and witnesses, animus of, to be exposed	ib.
—————————— to be sworn in any form binding on their consciences	ib.
—— to prove his case	ib.
bail should generally be accepted	ib.
hearsay evidence to be rejected	ib.
claims of British subjects, how to be advanced	98
—— put forward colourably under the name only of British subjects, not to be advanced	ib.
Consul should show to Authorities an example of strict impartiality	99
Interpreters to make written reports of the result of negotiations with Authorities	ib.
LUNACY, Supreme Court alone is a Court of	9

M

MATRIMONIAL CAUSES, Supreme Court alone can try,	9
MEDICAL OFFICERS serving on an Inquest, remuneration of	12
MERCHANT SHIPPING ACT, jurisdiction under, continued to Consuls	4
, under criminal sections of, cases are summary	37
MINISTER AT PEKIN, three Rules recently framed by, for—	
Registration of Bill of Sale	35, 102
Registration of Mortgages	ib. ib.
Suits against Partnerships and Agents	ib. ib.

	Page.
MINUTE OF PROCEEDINGS, Judge's, importance of ...	61
may be lent to parties in a suit, to obtain copies ...	22
must be drawn up in every case, civil and criminal	ib.
should be complete and accurate	ib.
MOTIONS TO SHOW CAUSE, ...	33
, an appeal from the Order on a, (if not *ex parte*), will lie to Supreme Court	34
record of, form of	ib.
, best course of procedure in	33
important statements to be made on oath	34
mode of hearing	ib.
to be made in writing	ib.
MUNICIPAL COUNCIL OF PORTS AND CONSULS, relations between	37
cases unprovided for by Municipal Regulations may come under the Law of England	38
coercive authority resides solely in Consul	ib.
Consul may, under Minister's authority, enforce Municipal Regulations	ib.
power and functions of Municipal Council derived from H. M.'s Minister	ib.
LAW OF ENGLAND, what it is,.........................	2

N

NATURALIZED BRITISH SUBJECTS, Chinese (or Japanese), have no right beyond the particular colony or possession	3
under what circumstances can be registered	20
, what are to be considered as	3
, when jurisdiction can be exercised over	ib.
NEW TRIALS	65
NOTES, JUDGE'S, see Minute of Proceedings.	
NOTIFICATION against British subjects of Chinese descent residing in the interior	101
of the publication of three Regulations for Registration..	ib.
on subject of Probate, 104; do. regarding Rowdies,	103

O

OATH administered to Coroner's Jury, form of..................	13
Witness at Inquest, form of	ib.
OBJECTION IN LAW	30
if established by Defendant, Plaintiff's case at once falls to the ground..	ib.
if not established, the case proceeds to trial	ib.
OFFENCES against Religion of country. how to be dealt with	18
—— the whole case to be reported to Supreme Court	19
, continuous, may be construed as misdemeanours...	ib.

[OFFENCES]
 on board British ship within 100 miles of coast, to be reported to Supreme Court 17
 · what rank under piracy.................. ib.
OFFENDER, CONVICTED, under what circumstances to be sent to Hongkong .... ib.
OFFICERS, CONSULAR, see CONSULAR OFFICERS.
OFFICIAL ADMINISTRATOR to property of deceased British subjects, in what cases and by whom appointed 15
ASSIGNEE, see BANKRUPT.
ORDER BEFORE SUIT, SUMMARY, extreme care required in 35
 IN COUNCIL is the authoritative guide for the Provincial Courts.................. 39
 , law of England to be followed in what is not expressly provided for by the .... ib.
 remarked on and explained as under:—
  Paragraph 9 of Preamble, page 3; section 3, ib.; ss. 4-6, p. 4; s. 25, ib.; ss. 26-32, p. 5; ss. 33-4, ib.; Subdivision V., ib.; s. 43, p. 8; ss. 43, 44, 46, p. 6; s. 47, ib.; ss. 48-50 (Reconciliation Clauses), ib.; ss. 49, 50, p. 9; s. 54, p. 14; ss. 57-61, p. 15; s. 60, p. 16; s. 62, p. 5; s. 63, ib.; ss. 64-80, p. 16; s. 77, p. 17; s. 79, ib.; s. 81, p. 20; s. 100, p. 18; s. 104, p. 19; s. 106, ib.; s. 113, p. 20; s. 114, ib.; s. 117, ib.; s. 143, p. 9; s. 146, p. 24; s. 148, ib.
 OF SEQUESTER, see SEQUESTER, ORDER OF.
 ON A MOTION, if not *ex parte*, an Appeal will lie to Supreme Court on 34
 ON JUDGMENT, see JUDGMENT ORDER.
 TO HOLD TO BAIL, see BAIL, ORDER TO HOLD TO.
ORDINANCES, &c., cannot be enacted by Consuls on their own responsibility 3
 , CONSULAR, what are not repealed .... ib.
  what are repealed .... ib.

P

PAPERS, FILING OF, should be systematic 27
PARTIES OUT OF JURISDICTION of Court, what course necessary.................. 29
 TO A CIVIL CASE may give evidence 23
PARTNER of a firm, death of, proper action by surviving Partners and by Consul in case of 16
PARTNERSHIP ESTATES, rule as to, in the case of the death of a Partner of the firm .... ib.
 OR AGENTS, Rule recently framed for suits against...35, 102
  Agent or Partner must be British subject 36

	Page.
PEACE, BREACHES OF THE, see BREACHES OF THE PEACE.	
PENALTY AND LIQUIDATED DAMAGES, distinction between	74
, instance of	ib.
FOR BREACH OF CONTRACT, see under DAMAGES.	
PERCENTAGE ON ESTATES of Deceased Persons, when chargeable by Consul	29
PERFORMANCE OF CONTRACTS, SPECIFIC	68
what is the best remedy for non-performance	69
PERSONAL ARREST, see ARREST OF THE PERSON.	
PETITION may be amended by Consul, if necessary	30
, nature of a	42
, service of	28
what is a bad	42
defective	ib.
ANSWER TO, may be amended by Consul	30
on oath	54
, procedure on	30, 52
should be short and relevant	43
where no answer put in, presumptions and proceedings in different cases	50
PIRACY, extended signification of	17
, punishment for	18
PLAINTS, entry of, example	28
, register of, form of	27
POSSESSION OF PREMISES, RECOVERY OF, see RECOVERY OF POSSESSION OF PREMISES.	
PRACTITIONERS	69
PREAMBLE TO "ORDER IN COUNCIL," paragraph 9 of, remarked on	3
PREMISES, RECOVERY OF POSSESSION OF, see RECOVERY OF POSSESSION OF PREMISES.	
PRINCIPAL OR AGENT, which? great care necessary	29
PROBATE, Circular Notification on subject of	104
contentious cases of, Supreme Court alone has jurisdiction in	9, 94
fees on	95
in the case of the death of a Partner of a firm	16
penalty on unauthorized persons dealing with an estate	95
, power of granting, to what cases confined	15
what is the proper action in other cases	16
, simple cases of, Consular Courts can act in	9
when party dies elsewhere than in China or Japan	16
PROCEDURE, RULES OF, see RULES OF PROCEDURE.	
PROCEEDINGS, BARRING	66
, COMPELLING	65
, INTERLOCUTORY, see INTERLOCUTORY PROCEEDINGS.	
ON DEATH of a British subject	15

	Page.
[PROCEEDINGS]	
———, RECORD OF, must be full and accurate...............	5
———, TERMINATING, provision for	66
PROPERTY OF DECEASED BRITISH SUBJECT, control exercised over, by Consular Officer only under authority of Supreme Court	15
Inventory of, when to be taken	ib.
———, Official Administrator of, appointed where necessary by Supreme Court only................................	ib.
vests in the first instance in Supreme Court	ib.
PROVINCIAL COURTS, CONSULAR, see CONSULAR COURTS.	
PUNISHMENT FOR PIRACY	18

Q

QUEEN'S (or KING'S) EVIDENCE, nature of..............	96
QUESTIONS OF ACCOUNTS may be referred	33
FACT OR LAW, reference of	26, 34
———, manner of procedure in	34
must be in writing..	ib.

R

RECONCILIATION CLAUSES in "Order in Council," remarked on	8, 40
RECORD, Courts of, what are...	5
of appeal from a decision on a Motion..................	34
———, of what it consists	22
———, original documents generally not to be forwarded	ib.
of Proceedings, must be full and accurate	5, 22
RECOVERY OF POSSESSION OF PREMISES.	
action on judgment	37
Act referred to	ib.
petition necessary	36
what necessary to establish defendant's case	37
plaintiff's case............	ib.
REFERENCE OF QUESTIONS for amicable settlement by Consuls	8
of account	33
of fact or law by consent	26, 34
———, manner of procedure in	34
must be put in writing	ib.
REGISTER OF PLAINTS, form of.............................	27
REGISTRATION	20
by British subjects at Foreign Consulates, consequence of...	ib.
Foreigners in British employ not to be registered ...	ib.
———, neglect of, how punished	ib.

	Page.
[REGISTRATION]	
BOOK, Consul's, form of	27
of Bankrupt's Estate must be kept	30
of Estate of Deceased Persons must be kept	29
OF BILLS OF SALE, Rule recently framed for.........35,	102
OF MORTGAGES, Rule recently framed for ....ib.,	ib.
RELIGION, OFFENCES AGAINST, how to be dealt with	18
whole case to be reported to Supreme Court	19
RETURNS, HALF-YEARLY, to be sent to Supreme Court	
by Consular Courts	8
ROWDIES, objectionableness of.............................	19
, Regulation providing for the surveillance of	103
, when and how the Court should act against	19
RULES recently framed by H. M.'s Minister at Pekin, three in number:—	
Registration of Bills of Sale 35,	102
Mortgages ....ib.,	ib.
Suits against Partnerships or Agents ....ib.,	ib.
OF PROCEDURE must be carefully complied with ...	21
, neglect in consulting	35
, object of	25
referred to or remarked on as under:—	

Nos. 1-9, pages 26, 34; 1-27, p. 25; 10-2, p. 41; 13-7, ib.; 18-25, ib.; 28, pp. 26, 28; 30-2, p. 26; 38, p. 29; 41, p. 27; 42, p. 28; 43, pp. 30, 43; 44-50, p. 25; 53, p. 30,; 55, pp. 30, 67; 56, p. 30; 58, pp. 25, 30, 33; 59, p. 9; 60-3, p. 30; 60-80, ib.; 64, p. 65; 74, p. 97; 77, p. 29; 84-94, p. 23; 95-8, p. 31; 99, pp. 6, 31; 105-15, p. 31; 109, ib.; 113, p. 32; 116-28, ib.; 129-36, ib.; 131, pp. 32, 33; 134, p. 32; 138, p. 33; 138-9, p. 32; 144-52, p. 33; Subdivision VI., ib.; 145, p. 22; 145, 4th paragraph, p. 34; 149-51, ib.; 153, ib.; 153-82, p. 21; 154-62, p. 32; 155, ib.; 163-74, p. 31; 170, p. 22; 175-8, p. 34; 179, p. 35; 179-82, p. 45; 184-216, p. 15; 217-29, pp. 9, 21; 230-42, pp. 34, 35; 248, p. 23; 252, p. 36; 254-9, p. 7; 254-60, p. 28; 257, p. 7; 261, p. 45; 262-3, p. 24; 274, p. 31; 275, p. 26.

S

SECURITY, how much to be taken, from whom, and what kind	6, 19
SEQUESTER, ORDER OF	46
action as to stoppage *in transitu*	ib.
when to be granted	ib.
SERVICE OF PETITION 28,	48
at the last place of residence, when to be resorted to	7, 48
-book should be kept by Serving Officer	28
, in what cases the plaintiff may serve	48

	Page.
[SERVICE OF PETITION]	
, proceedings after	49
, substituted	48
SETTLEMENT OF ISSUES	30
, the Court may of itself settle the issues	50
SHIPPING ACT, MERCHANT, see MERCHANT SHIPPING ACT.	
SHIPS, STOPPAGE OF, see STOPPAGE OF SHIPS.	
SPECIAL CASES, provided for by Rule 99	6, 31
, referred to Supreme Court	31
SPECIFIC PERFORMANCE OF CONTRACTS	68
what is the best remedy in cases of non-performance	69
STOPPAGE OF SHIPS	47
, agent to be applied to	ib.
cases in which Agent may be unwilling to act	ib.
ships under charters not to be stopped	ib.
SUITS AGAINST PARTNERSHIPS AND AGENTS, Rule recently framed for	35, 102
Partner or Agent must be British subject	36
, CROSS	67
LONG PENDING, how to be terminated	66
SUMMARY CASES, civil and criminal, to be conducted formally	37
(civil) and indictment cases, distinction to be observed between	95
ORDERS before Suit	35
extreme care required	ib.
PROCEDURE, certain cases of	41
SUMMONS for Coroner's Jury, form of	12
issuing into another Consular district, form of	7
, great caution required in	ib.
JUDGMENT, see JUDGMENT SUMMONS.	
SUPREME COURT alone can hold Jury trials	5
alone has admiralty jurisdiction	14
, decision by, on a special point	31
, functions of	9
has extraordinary original jurisdiction over China and Japan, concurrent with Provincial Courts	5, 40
, Judges of, may order cases to be tried at Shanghai	ib., ib.
may visit ports to try cases (criminal cases especially)	ib., ib.
may issue Order of Execution to Provincial Court	8
APPEAL TO, see APPEAL TO SUPREME COURT.	
SURVEYS by Experts	24
generally have little legal force	ib.
on unimportant subjects should be discouraged	ib.
when necessary	ib.

T

TERMINATING LONG PENDING SUITS, provision for	66
TEXT-BOOKS on International Law, recommended	2

	Page.
[TEXT-BOOKS]	
on Law, recommended	2
TREATIES AND REGULATIONS	17
TRIALS BY JURY can be held only by the Supreme Court	5
, NEW	13

V

VERDICT OF CORONER'S JURY	65

W

WARRANT OF ARREST in criminal cases, when to be resorted to	95
in debt cases, under what circumstances permitted	33
WITNESSES at Inquest, form of Oath for	13
, competency of, what are valid objections to the	57
, cross-examination of, permitted only on material points	62
, depositions of, may be taken when the witness is about to leave the place	56
, examination of,	23
, expenses of,	24
in what cases to be allowed	ib.
for the accused, summonses should be granted for the	96
of different creeds, how to be sworn	13
of different nationalities, attendance of, how to be secured	13, 56
, presence of, in what cases not compellable by warrant	96
, sufficient notice to be given to	56
WRITS, EXECUTION OF, care to be exercised in the	6

www.ingramcontent.com/pod-product-compliance
Lightning Source LLC
Chambersburg PA
CBHW021350230426
43666CB00006B/472